PRESCRIPTION FOR CONFLICT

PRESCRIPTION FOR CONFLICT

ISRAEL'S WEST BANK SETTLEMENT POLICY

Merle Thorpe, Jr.

Foreword Amnon Kapeliuk

Introduction Simha Flapan

FOUNDATION FOR MIDDLE EAST PEACE

1984

Copyright © 1984 by Foundation for Middle East Peace.
All rights reserved.
Printed in the United States of America.
International Standard Book Number 0-9613707-0-X
Library of Congress Card Catalog Number 84-081545
Library of Congress Cataloging in Publications Data
Prescription for Conflict:
Israel's West Bank Settlement Policy
Thorpe, Merle Jr.
Foreword: Amnon Kapeliuk
Introduction: Simha Flapan

FOUNDATION FOR MIDDLE EAST PEACE

1522 K Street, N.W., Suite 202, Washington, D.C. 20005

This book is dedicated to those many Israelis, Palestinians and Jews world wide, who seek peace and security for Israelis and Palestinians through mutual recognition and a division of the contested land.

CONTENTS

APPENDICES

PREFACE

THE ISRAELI-PALESTINIAN CONFLICT, marked by frequent wars and human suffering, continues to grip the Middle East. For many reasons, among them our commitment to Israel and the risk of nuclear war, Americans should consider the peaceful resolution of the conflict a matter of the highest priority.

The future of the West Bank and the Gaza Strip remains the central issue in this conflict. Will these territories be absorbed into the Jewish State of Israel? Or will they become a physical homeland for the more than one million Palestinians who live there, and a psychological homeland for the more than three million Palestinians in the Palestinian diaspora?

The present Israeli government is dedicated to an *Eretz Yisrael,* or "Greater Israel," implying an indissoluble, eternally non-negotiable bond to these territories. Israel has been attempting to discredit the idea of Palestinian nationalism or to force world opinion to focus on Jordan as the Palestinian state. A growing number of Jews in Israel and in Jewish communities worldwide, as well as many others, however, consider this attitude inimical to Jewish values and contrary to Israel's long-term security interests. A considerable body of world opinion considers this attitude a prescription for permanent war between Israel and the Arab world. Israeli policies, moreover, seriously undermine both the United Nations General Assembly partition plan adopted in 1947 and the *Camp David Accords.*(The Accords called for fulfilling "the legitimate rights of the Palestinian people" with a five-year transition period from Israeli rule in the occupied territories.)

The strong commitment Americans feel toward Israel reflects admiration for the Jewish people and for their contribution to western civilization. It is a commitment that deplores centuries of anti-Semitism—above all the unparalleled treatment of Jews during World War II. So strong is this commitment that it has tended to restrict criticism of Israel and Israeli policies. In the Jewish community the reluctance to criticize derives from a fear that any criticism will play into the hands of Israel's enemies. Other persons fear that their criticism may be construed as generally anti-Semitic.

This work focuses on Israel's plan for the Jewish settlement of the West Bank, and seeks to explain its devastating effect on prospects for peace. It is also important for Americans to understand that our government's aid to Israel assists the Israeli government in pursuing this plan, and that the United States therefore shares responsibility for its immediate as well as long-term effects.

The high price the U.S. pays for helping to finance as well as to give political support to Israel's military occupation of the West Bank and to its settlement program is illustrated by the results of a poll of West Bank Palestinians. The poll was commissioned by *Time* magazine and conducted in the spring of 1982 (prior to the invasion of Lebanon) by scholars at an Israeli research institute. Seventy-two percent of the Palestinians polled said that, as between the Soviet Union and the U.S., the Soviet Union was the "more admired," while only 1.6 percent named the United States.* This result does not reflect an innate West Bank sympathy with Communism; it reveals, simply, the feelings of West Bank Palestinians. They are convinced that the U.S. is indirectly responsible for the occupation and for the denial of their liberties. Such anti-American sentiment on the part of a people who have attained the highest level of education of any people in the Arab world cannot be in America's interest. Unfortunately, similar anti-Americanism, stimulated by perceived American biases, has also spread to many other countries in the Middle East.

Recently, many prominent Jewish leaders in both the U.S. and Israel have spoken out against American policies toward Israel. Eugene B. Borowitz, Professor of Jewish Philosophy at the Hebrew Union College in New York, and editor of *Sh'ma*, the well-known journal of Jewish studies, has written:

> And we surely cannot expect our American Jewish lobbying groups to now start discriminating as to which issues they will or won't put their/our full weight behind. They exist to carry the fight for the State of Israel and to have no independent basis upon which to evaluate or resist its demands upon us. Similarly, most of our American Jewish organizations are by now such hostages to the State of Israel that they can only hesitantly be expected to face such serious questions as now need to be raised.**

Similarly Mattityahu Peled, Professor of Arabic Studies at the University of Tel Aviv who was a Major General and member of the General Staff of the Israeli Defense Forces, has posed a relevant question:

> Only recently have Americans become aware of the considerable body of Israelis who watch the United States' enormous financial support of our

---

* *Time*, May 24, 1982.
** Eugene B. Borowitz, *Sh'ma*, December 25, 1981.

country with growing misgivings. . . . I, for one, would also like to ask the American taxpayer: 'Why are you giving us the rope with which to hang ourselves?'*

The Foreword by Amnon Kapeliuk and the Introduction by Simha Flapan provide readers particularly insightful perspectives on the conflict. Mr. Flapan has had a distinguished career as an Israeli author and editor while Dr. Kapeliuk is an equally respected Israeli journalist and author. Both are dedicated to their country and its security and believe Israel's policies toward Palestinians to be in the interest of neither Israel nor the Jewish people. Both have a particular concern that Israel's supporters in the U.S. be informed about the conflict and actively interest themselves in its resolution.

Merle Thorpe, Jr., *President*
Foundation for Middle East Peace

Washington, D.C.
April, 1984

---

* Mattityahu Peled, "Too Much U.S. Rope," *The New York Times*, December 30, 1982.

FOREWORD

THE ISRAELI SETTLEMENTS ON THE WEST BANK are among the principal obstacles to the resolution of the Israeli-Arab conflict—particularly the Israeli-Palestinian question. This fact was vividly illustrated by the prolonged Israeli-Egyptian negotiations which took place from December 1977 to March 1979 regarding Israeli settlements in the Sinai. The Egyptians were willing to sign a peace treaty only after an explicit agreement calling for the Sinai settlements to be dismantled—including the town of Yamit—was exacted. That same process will have to be repeated in the occupied Palestinian territories—the West Bank and the Gaza Strip. While it might be possible for the settlements to be left standing, it is clear that no Arab-Palestinian peace negotiators will agree to leave these settlements under Israeli sovereignty. They will probably have to be subject to a new sovereign power—either Palestinian or Jordanian-Palestinian. It is equally apparent that additional settlements are only further obstacles to the achievement of a just peace.

The subject is being clouded by innumerable fixed notions, deliberately fostered illusions and outright lies. One proposition is that Israel has the right to establish these settlements and that they are "harmless". According to international law, however, lands seized in the course of war restrict the occupiers' right to them. Contrary to this law the Knesset voted to annex first East Jerusalem and later the Golan Heights. (It has not yet annexed the West Bank and the Gaza Strip.)

When the government sought to expropriate a Jordanian-owned electricity company which serves East Jerusalem and the West Bank, the issue was brought before the Israeli High Court of Justice. In early 1981 the High Court determined that the West Bank is an occupied territory temporarily subject to military rule and, therefore, that "the local military government is subject to the international laws concerning military occupation, unless the latter plainly conflicted with local law." In barring the expropriation of the electricity company's installations, the High Court decreed that "the acts of the occupying power in the occupied territories must be confined to effecting non-permanent changes. Permanent changes may be made only in the absence of any other feasible course of action."

Shortly after the Six-Day War when the first settlements were established, the official view of the ruling Labour government was that these were security measures, and thus in accordance with international law. Within a few years it became clear that these were, indeed, civilian settlements intended to be permanent. This, then, was a preliminary move to the outright annexation of the area and thus an obvious violation of Article 6 of the Geneva Convention (August 12, 1949). (Art. 6, concerned with the defense of civilian populations in time of war, states that "the occupying power may not transfer parts of its own civilian population to the territory under occupation".) The international jurist, Professor Joram Dinstein, concurs. In his recent work, *The Laws of War,* he points out that Israel's settlements, destruction of homes and deportation of Palestinian inhabitants are all in violation of international law.

Despite this, there is a unilateral movement of Israelis, with full protection of the Israeli armed forces, into the occupied territories. Those responsible for the settlements speak and act as if the entire area between the Mediterranean Sea and the Jordan River belongs exclusively to the Jewish people.

Leaders of the Likud bloc led by former Prime Minister Menachem Begin have repeatedly declared that the settlements are deliberately being established in areas densely populated by Arabs so as to prevent any future consideration of Israeli withdrawal. They are thus not only illegal but are obstructive to any negotiated peace.

Supporters of settlements also argue that the close proximity of Jewish and Arab populations in the West Bank is conducive to peaceful coexistence. This is patently untrue. An apartheid-like regime is developing where the two populations live side by side, but where the Jewish settlers have more rights (in some cases even more than the citizens of Israel within its borders) and enjoy the protection of the army. The Palestinians, by contrast, have no political and civil rights and are subject to the arbitrary will of the army and the settlers. The settlers there participate in the political process in Israel while the Arabs are deprived even of the right to elect their own municipal councils. Many of the mayors who were elected to office in 1976 (the last time municipal elections were held in the occupied territories) have been deposed or even deported by the military authorities. They were replaced by Israeli civilian appointees or army officers. The Jews living there are subject to Israeli law while the Palestinians are subject to Jordanian and /or to Israeli military law. The maintenance of these two distinct legal systems is clearly undemocratic.

If there were any truth to the Likud's declared aim of "peaceful coexistence" between Arabs and Jews in the West Bank, then surely the least suitable Jewish group, so far as proximity to the Arab population is concerned, is the *Gush Emunim* ("Block of the Faithful"). They regard the Palestinians as aliens and make no secret that their ultimate goal is to expel them altogether. In the publication, *Nekudah,* a settler from Kedumin could write:

> If we want to have a future, then there is no room for Arabs in this country. . . . The way of coexistence is dangerous, and if we continue along it we will reach a state when our lives will be in danger. When that happens there will be no choice but to put the Arabs on buses and send them across the bridges.*

The settlers also act as if they are entirely above the reach of the law. They form vigilante groups, destroy property, wound, and even kill local Palestinians. In the years 1982 and 1983 some one dozen West Bank Palestinian civilians were killed by Jewish settlers. Another twenty Palestinian civilians were killed by the armed forces in the course of clashes. Whenever Jewish property or persons are injured by Palestinians, the military and security forces invariably bring the culprits to justice, but the authorities do not display the same diligence in dealing with the persistant harrassment and violence perpetrated by settlers. In 1980 dozens of vehicles and shop fronts in the West Bank towns of Ramallah and Al Bireh were destroyed. Although that infamous "night of the shattered panes" was known to have been perpetrated by some settlers of Beth El II, no one was charged. Recently, two former chiefs of Israeli security, Avraham Ahituv and Issar Harel, have expressed the opinion that there is even an anti-Palestinian Jewish underground operating in the West Bank.

Knesset member Shulamit Aloni, of the *Citizens' Rights Movement* which is a part of the *Labour Alignment,* and who is well known for her concern for civil rights, has drawn our attention to the fact that:

> Since 1967 we have become the conquerors of the Palestinian population. The authorities flout international conventions concerning the rights of civilian populations under occupation, violate their basic human rights, apply collective punishment and have made it a regular policy to subject the inhabitants to degradation. The *Likud* government's policy of occupation and annexation founded on national-religious principles has reached its most extreme manifestation in the orders and tacit authorization of inexcusable acts given by Minister of Defence Ariel Sharon and Chief of Staff Raphael Eitan.

Testifying before a miliary tribunal, Chief of Staff Rafael Eitan admitted:

---

*Nekudah, December 23, 1983.

Indeed we are using collective punishment in the occupied territories. There is also a standing order to punish the parents of juvenile rioters.

At the same tribunal, Major David Mofaz revealed that he had been ordered:

to round up men between the ages of 18 and 26, and even high school boys, bring them to the local school, shut them in the classrooms and bring in soldiers with truncheons to hit them on their legs and their wristwatches, as this was both painful and a loss of property.

Other forms of collective punishment against Arab civilians have included the demolition of the homes of those suspected of armed assault against either Israeli civilians or military personnel and curfews placed on Palestinian villages and towns. (To date 2,300 houses have been demolished.) The inhabitants of Hebron, Deharieh and the refugee camp of Deheysheh were placed under such a curfew with only brief intervals to procure food. The detainees continue to complain of torture during interrogations. (Since 1977 when the *Sunday Times* [London] published information on torture in the occupied territories, conditions have improved.) In addition, the authorities routinely suspend the functioning of Palestinian schools, colleges and universities whose members actively struggle against the occupation.

Many of these repressive measures, based on the so-called *Emergency Defense Regulations* promulgated in 1945 during the British Mandate, were used ironically against the Jewish community during their own struggle for independence. In February 1948 the Bar Association of the Jewish community in Palestine convened to protest these regulations, and its president went so far as to condemn them as "an outright violation of the principles of law, equity and justice. . . ." Amnesty International has also registered its disapproval—asserting that the population of the occupied territories are being punished for their beliefs rather than for crimes committed.

Another area of grave concern is land expropriation. Today, two-thirds of the total land area of the West Bank is in Israeli hands. This includes land belonging to private individuals whose proper registration, due to the slowness of the land registry offices during British and Jordanian times, was faulty and inadequate. The authorities have hastened to claim these lands and define them as "public," *i.e.,* available for use by the governing power. Other lands have simply been expropriated or purchased under coercive conditions. "Of all the blows we have received at the hands of the occupiers," says Bassam Shak'a, the deposed mayor of Nablus, "the hardest is the expropriation of our land." Palestinian residents whose land has been expropriated and turned over to settlements have repeatedly petitioned the High Court of Justice, but to date the Court has annulled only one such transaction. When the courts held up certain land transactions to examine whether proper procedures were followed, the Israeli military commander in July 1983 issued an unprecedented order (No. 1060) depriving the Israeli civil courts of their jurisdiction over land disputes. Today, an appeals commission composed of three Israeli officials deals with these disputes. In this way the military authorities circumvent the law, leaving the Palestinian inhabitants without recourse to a civil legal authority.

Supporters of the settlements also argue that the living standard of West Bank Palestinians has risen. There is no doubt that the level of consumption has, in fact, increased but the local economy has also been made exceedingly vulnerable to outside factors. It is almost wholly dependent on the Israeli economy which it has been made to serve. The government has invested hundreds of millions of dollars in the settlements and in their infrastructure. Some of this is derived from direct U.S. aid and some from tax-deductible contributions sent by Jews overseas. The local economy of the West Bank, however, does not receive any funds for development, nor does its relationship with the economy of Israel permit independent growth.

In a recent report on human rights in the West Bank and Gaza,* it was revealed that as far back as the mid-1970s the government had decided not to invest in the development of productive industries in the territories. The authorities also placed innumerable bureaucratic obstacles in the path of Palestinian developers who wanted to invest in new industries. Similarly, while Israeli banks operate widely throughout the territories, the government has barred the establishment of Arab banks capable of sustaining an independent credit system for the benefit of the local population. In 1980 the government fund which is used to extend credit for development was closed. There is now no central economic authority in the West Bank to manage the economy for the benefit of its inhabitants.

Worst of all, the Palestinian inhabitants are prevented from protecting their own goods: the economy, which is technologically and industrially far less advanced than that of Israel, is exposed to a flood of Israeli products with which the Palestinian agriculturalists and industrialists cannot possibly compete. This advantage is carefully maintained by the military government. Thus, on the one hand, when the local farmers encounter difficulties in marketing their produce across the Jordan River and wish to market in Israel, the authorities impose restrictions designed to protect Israeli farmers. On the other, the agricultural as well

Human Rights In The Occupied Territories 1979-1983 (Tel Aviv: International Center for Peace in the Middle East, November 1983).

as industrial goods produced by the Jewish settlements receive massive support from the government and the Jewish Agency. With similar discrimination, the water allowance to the Palestinian farmer is only about a third of that to the settlements.* The military authority has abandoned virtually all responsibility for local services, except those for the settlements.

The apartheid-like system in the territories is also reflected in the status of the workers. The Jewish settlers enjoy the same status and rights as Israeli workers, whereas the Palestinian workers (representing nine percent of the manpower in Israel) are a source of cheap, unprotected labor. An Arab worker from the West Bank employed inside Israel, for example, cannot obtain tenure, and is grossly discriminated against in matters of social security, sick funds and leave time. His wages are neither as high as those of his Israeli counterpart nor does he enjoy the protection of Israeli labor unions.

Settlement construction is accelerating, as if in a race against time. The government is anxious to create the impression that the future of the West Bank has already been decided: the Palestinians will simply have to accept this as they had to accept conditions laid down in 1948-49 (when portions of the Mandate the UN had designated as the Arab state were annexed by Israel).

The difference between these periods, however, is considerable. Following the 1948-49 war, there was an international consensus concerning the territorial facts created by the war. The Arab states signed armistice agreements with Israel defining the new lines of demarcation and the Arab inhabitants of Israel received Israeli nationality. In January 1949 they voted for the first Knesset and were even elected to it. In the years that followed not one major power demanded that Israel withdraw to the 1947 partition lines.

By contrast, in the seventeen years since the Six-Day War, not a single country including the U.S. has recognized the new boundaries of "Greater Israel". Moderate Palestinians, however, are willing to enter negotiations with Israel on the basis of former armistice boundaries.

Most important, the entire Arab population of the West Bank, without exception, is firmly opposed to the occupation. Even the inhabitants of East Jerusalem have desisted from asking for Israeli citizenship, although it was offered to them freely. (Out of one hundred thousand Arab Jerusalemites, only a few hundred have availed themselves of the offer.) Thus, while confederation with Jordan might be considered, they will not settle for less than self-determination, which includes an independent state in their own homeland.

*Agence France Presse 27 December 1983

Begin's so-called "Autonomy Plan" is both utopian and deceptive since it was meant to be applied only to the people and not to the land. Its purpose was to create two separate political-legal systems in the same territory, and the settlements were designed to advance this program. Today the Israeli people are beginning to experience a disenchantment with the settlements. In late 1983 the widely-read daily, *Ha'aretz*, published a poll revealing that 48.5 percent of the persons questioned were opposed to the establishment of additional settlements. (In October 1981 only 29.2 percent were opposed.) When divided into social-educational strata, it seems that the higher the level of education the greater the opposition to the settlements. Among university-educated people about 55 percent are now opposed to them.

It is increasingly clear that the Israeli government's policies can only lead our nation to a dead end.

Amnon Kapeliuk

Jerusalem
February, 1984

DR. AMNON KAPELIUK is an Israeli journalist and trained Arabist. His father emigrated from the Ukraine to Palestine during the British Mandate. Dr. Kapeliuk is a graduate of the Asia-Africa Institute of the Hebrew University and the Sorbonne. He is a correspondent for the Israeli daily *Al Hamishmar* and for *Le Monde*. He has published books on the Yom Kippur War (1973) and on the Sabra and Shatilla massacre, the latter reprinted in seven languages.

INTRODUCTION

This work reflects the deep-seated anguish and moral outrage felt by many Israeli and Diaspora Jews towards the Israeli government's drive to accelerate the construction of Jewish settlements in the West Bank and Gaza. This policy, which is an annexation of the Arab territories in Palestine in all but name, can be implemented only by force. It generates a vicious cycle of violence that dehumanizes and brutalizes Arab-Jewish relations.

The so-called "liberal occupation" of the West Bank which, it was claimed, would promote the welfare, social progress, and economic development of the Palestinian community there, has become a regime of oppression. Palestinian resistance to the confiscation of their land and economic resources and to the absolute control of the Israeli military administration over their lives is suppressed by the dismissal of democratically-elected mayors, by house arrests and censorship, by the prohibition of all political and cultural activities motivated by national aspirations, and by the collective punishment of entire villages and towns. Hardly a day passes without Arab strikes, stone-throwing and demonstrations that even armed force cannot contain.

Israel has lost its image as a state aspiring to peace and democracy. The violation of elementary human and national rights of the Palestinians has lent credibility to the propaganda that equates Zionism with racism, colonialism, apartheid, and military expansionism.

The attitude of Diaspora Jewry towards these policies has been one of self-imposed silence accompanied by continued financial and political support. It is argued that Diaspora Jews have no right to interfere in security matters and in the internal policies of a democratically-elected government of the Jewish state.

This argument is historically inaccurate, politically incorrect, and morally wrong.

The State of Israel was not established by and for Israelis alone. It was built by a world Zionist movement that claimed to represent the historical interests of the whole Jewish people. Indeed, it was the Jewish Agency that negotiated with the United Nations over the rights of the

23

Jewish settlers in Palestine, the conflict with the Palestinian people, and the future of the whole country. The Agency itself was recognized in the Mandate of Palestine and by the League of Nations as a public body authorized to act on behalf of all the Jewish people in matters affecting the establishment of a Jewish national home.

After the outbreak of violence in 1936, the Jewish Agency repeatedly declared its commitment to the principle of non-domination. While it insisted on Jewish rights to statehood and sovereignty, the Agency stressed its recognition of the rights of the Palestinian Arabs. It was this body, which included such eminent representatives of World Jewry as Dr. Emmanuel Newman, Rabbi Abba Hillel Silver, Rose Halprin, Dr. Haim Greenberg, Dr. Nahum Goldmann and Dr. Chaim Weizmann, that later, in 1947, adopted the United Nations General Assembly partition plan for the resolution of the conflict.

In May 1947 Rabbi Silver, on behalf of the Agency, told the United Nations Special Committee on Palestine (UNSCOP):

> When we speak of a Jewish State we do not have in mind any racial or theocratic state but one which will be based on full equality and rights for all inhabitants without distinction of religion or race and without domination or subjugation.

And shortly afterward David Ben-Gurion, Chairman of the Agency, echoed his sentiments:

> We are bringing homeless and persecuted Jews to our country and settling them in Jewish towns and villages *not in Arab areas*. It never entered our minds to charge the Arabs with solving the Jewish problem. . . .

When Moshe Shertok (Sharett), Director of the Agency's Political Department, urged UNSCOP to implement "unlimited immigration of Jewish refugees to Palestine," he specified that it be on condition that they "not displace or worsen the lot of the existing inhabitants who are also there as of right."

It was this recognition of Palestinian rights that led the Agency and the World Zionist Organization (WZO) to accept the idea of partition and the establishment of a Palestinian state alongside a Jewish state. When WZO voted, 51 to 16, in September 1947, to accept UNSCOP's partition recommendation, the 16 votes against partition included ten votes of two socialist parties, *Hashomer Hatzair,* which favored a bi-national state, and *Achdut Avodah,* which proposed an international trusteeship. Thus only six votes, representing the Revisionist Party led by Vladimir Jabotinsky (Menachem Begin's teacher and founder of Begin's *Herut* party), opposed the historical decision of the Jewish people to establish their own sovereign state on a non-discriminatory basis and *not* at the expense of Palestinian national rights.

That the Arab state never materialized was due to the extremism of the Palestinian leadership at the time. This myopic leadership engaged its people and the Arab states in a war that brought calamity upon them. The Palestinians became refugees—living in camps and dispersed over the whole region. Part of their territory was annexed by Israel and Jordan. The idea of a contiguous Palestinian state peacefully coexisting with Israel, though, did not vanish with the end of the 1948 war. In negotiations between Israel and the Arab states in 1949 and in 1950 (within the framework of the UN Palestinian Commission), many Israeli leaders viewed the establishment of a Palestinian state as more desirable for the security of Israel than the incorporation of the West Bank into Transjordan. Serious and prolonged debates took place in the Knesset—the General Zionists, Mapam and the Independent Liberals opposing annexation by Transjordan.

After the War of Independence in 1948, many people thought that the exodus of the Palestinians from the areas taken over by the IDF in the war was what Dr. Chaim Weizmann described as a "miraculous simplification". They believed it liberated Israel from the complex problem of securing the land and ensuring equality for a very large Arab population. In fact, the exodus and ensuing refugee problem became the major factor that undermined cease-fire and armistice attempts and prevented peace between Israel and the Arab states. It generated an endless cycle of sabotage, terror and massive retaliation. It stimulated an arms race and military confrontations.

Dispersed, the Palestinian refugees wandered throughout the Arab world carrying with them the anguish and horror they suffered in the wars. Arab fears and hatred of Israel were exacerbated. The Palestinians were able to exploit these feelings, as well as internal tensions within Arab countries, to strengthen Arab unity. They hoped these conditions would eventually force Israel to restore their property and rights.

After the occupation of the West Bank in 1967, many prominent Israeli leaders, including the President of Israel, Chaim Herzog, sought to establish a Palestinian state on the West Bank, which would be the first Arab nation to sign a peace treaty with Israel. The initiative was rejected—not by the West Bank leadership, many of whom were ready to enter into negotiations, but by the Israeli Cabinet. Unfortunately, it was not only Menachem Begin's pressure for the annexation of the West Bank that killed this initiative. The intoxication of many Labor leaders with the swift and seemingly decisive military victory led them to believe in the possibility of new strategic borders.

The policy of achieving these frontiers *unilaterally* by creating *faits accomplis*—Jewish settlements in the occupied territories—obfuscated the ideological differences between Labor and Liberal Zionism on the one hand and Revisionist Zionism on the other. The latter has always aimed at a "Greater Israel" in the whole of Palestine to be achieved if necessary by force. The erosion of the ideas and values of Labor and Liberal Zionism paved the way for Begin's party to come to power. This transition marked a radical change in Israel's position in the world, and also affected World Jewry.

The Begin government launched a feverish effort to change the demographic, economic and political structure of the West Bank in a way that would make its incorporation into the state irreversible. A "Greater Israel," extending to its so-called historic boundaries, was an imperative to be achieved even at the high cost of renouncing a commitment, maintained by the Jewish people for more than half a century, to the rights of the Palestinian people. The government sought to fulfill its vision even if it led to the erosion of the moral values from which Israel draws its strength or worse, to the total collapse of the peace process in the Middle East and to Israel's isolation in the world community.

The government tries to justify its policy by arguing that a Palestinian state would be the paramount threat to Israel's security. This view, however, was seriously undermined by the war in Lebanon where a Palestinian "state" bent on *irredentist* guerrilla warfare was liquidated by the IDF in two days, with few casualties. It is not easy to reconcile Israel's overpowering military and technological superiority with fear of a small hypothetical state lacking a modern economy and territorial contiguity. The security argument of a "narrow waist" can impress only those ignorant of modern warfare and technology. It is not topography and borders, but superiority of firepower, airpower, mobility, and capacity for counter-offense or preemptive action that guarantees victory.

The war in Lebanon, in all its tragic dimensions, was a direct consequence of the policy of annexation of the West Bank. All along, the government has sought to create a collaborationist leadership to acquiesce in massive Jewish settlement and to accept a miserly autonomy. To assist this, Begin had to try to liquidate the PLO as a military and alternative political force that could exert influence on the West Bank.

But the war did not liquidate the PLO, nor did the rebellion within the fighting units of Al-Fatah abolish the support of the overwhelming majority in the Palestinian movement for Arafat. The rebels, despite their Syrian support, cannot provide an alternative to his leadership. The overwhelming majority—if not all—of Palestinians in the West Bank and Gaza are on his side. He symbolizes a political solution to their struggle for independence.

The destruction of the Palestinian self-governing authority in Lebanon with its schools, hospitals, social welfare, cultural and economic enterprises and the continued homelessness, dispersion, refugee status, and discrimination Palestinians suffer at the hand of both Arabs and Israelis only intensifies and reinforces Palestinian determination for independence and a normal life.

The West Bank and the Gaza Strip have now become the central focus for a national revival that will give the Palestinian people freedom and equality. The Palestinians in the West Bank have become the focal point of their national movement. They are demonstrating a political maturity characterized by both radicalism and realism. Radicalism is reflected by their determination to develop their land, culture, and national institutions. Realism is reflected by their refusal to engage in acts of indiscriminate terror which would serve as an excuse to remove them from their land. They have no illusions about the aims of the Israeli government, the crisis in the PLO and the powerlessness of the Arab world, and they recognize Israel's strength and vitality and the futility of seeking to destroy it. At the same time they are conscious of their responsibility to the Palestinian people whose national revival and independence depends on their ability to preserve their will and aspirations. Though conditions are desperate, their mood is not one of despair, and they are strengthened by the knowledge that there are considerable forces inside Israel struggling for democracy, human rights and peace.

If the Palestinian right to self-determination is recognized, there is little doubt that Arafat and the overwhelming majority of Palestinian Arabs living under Israeli occupation would be ready to negotiate a peace settlement with Israel.

If this right is denied, the inevitable consequence will be a new, prolonged period of violence in which even Israel's technological and military superiority will not guarantee peace and security. Deprived of political freedom and a national, cultural, and economic infrastructure, Palestinian aspirations will express themselves in the emergence of uncontrollable groups of "suicide fighters" engaged in desperate acts of terror against those held responsible. It is a historical fact that this kind of terror can hardly be prevented even by highly organized and powerful states. The continuation of Israeli rule and oppression in the West Bank will thus ruin the last chance for a peaceful resolution to the conflict. It is also the road to Israel's self-destruction.

The circle of violence caused by resistance and oppression leads to an erosion of Israeli moral and social values and to the emergence of fanatic, chauvinist, terrorist elements that defy the authority of the state's jurisprudence and government, destroy Israeli democracy, and erode the unity and solidarity of the Jewish people.

The dangers involved in this process cannot be exaggerated. It deepens Arab hostility and hatred, confirming past fears and suspicions of Zionism and justifying the continuing struggle against the Jewish state. It erases Gentile feelings of guilt and shame for their feeble efforts to prevent the Holocaust, and it paralyzes the friends of Israel who combat anti-Semitism but cannot do it by defending Israel's policy of annexation, oppression, and violation of human rights. It splits the unity of the Jewish people who remain living as national minorities and cannot accept the double standard of struggling for human rights of Jews, while at the same time justifying the violation of these very rights for Palestinians. Above all, it creates a state of turbulence in the region which endangers peace and stability—not only in the Middle East, but in the world at large.

Anti-Israeli views and sentiments can easily become anti-Jewish feelings that strengthen anti-Semitism. The most dangerous phenomenon, however, lies in the fact that anti-Israeli feelings and attitudes develop now not among the backward elements of society, whose racial and religious prejudices can be diverted from their real social problems into anti-Jewish outbursts, but among the most educated, liberal, and progressive segments of public opinion—those who struggle for justice, equality, social progress, and peace.

The only way to save Israel from this degeneration is to put an end to its rule over the Palestinian people. The recognition of their right to self-determination and statehood will open the way to mutual recognition, coexistence, and a comprehensive peace. This is a task which Diaspora Jewry cannot evade if it wants Israel to survive as a democratic Jewish state and as a cultural center for the whole Jewish people. An alliance with the Israeli peace camp struggling for a fundamental change of policy is therefore the most urgent political duty of every Jew concerned with Israel's security and future.

Simha Flapan

Tel Aviv
February, 1984

SIMHA FLAPAN was born in Poland and emigrated to Palestine in 1930. A former member of Kibbutz Gan Shmuel and Director of Arab Affairs (Mapalm), he was also for twenty-four years Editor-in-Chief of the Israeli monthly, *New Outlook*. He is the author of *Zionism and the Palestinians*, and in 1982 received the Kreisky Foundation Human Rights Award in recognition of his efforts on behalf of Israeli-Palestinian peace.

I. *Background to the Conflict*

THE ZIONIST MOVEMENT FOR A JEWISH STATE in Palestine had its origins in Theodore Herzl's pamphlet, *The Jewish State*, published in 1896. The most significant milestone in the movement, however, was the Balfour Declaration of late 1917, in which Arthur James Balfour, the British foreign secretary, informed the second Lord Rothschild that:

> His Majesty's Government view with favour the establishment in Palestine of a national home for the Jewish people, and will use their best endeavours to facilitate the achievement of this object, it being clearly understood that nothing shall be done which may prejudice the civil and religious rights of existing non-Jewish communities in Palestine, or the rights and political status enjoyed by Jews in any other country.*

Article 22 of the *Covenant of the League of Nations* specified that:

> To those colonies and territories which as a consequence of the late war have ceased to be under the sovereignty of the States which formerly governed them. . . . there should be applied the principle that the well-being and development of [their] peoples form a sacred trust of civilization. . . .

It further provided that "the tutelage of such peoples shall be entrusted to advanced nations" and "exercised by them as Mandatories on behalf of the League."[1]

Ottoman Empire territories were transferred thereafter by peace treaty to the Allied Powers who conferred a mandate for Palestine on the United Kingdom. The Mandate, which incorporated the principles of the Balfour Declaration, was subsequently approved by the League of Nations on July 24, 1922. In September 1922 Transjordan, the territory east of the Jordan River, was removed from the purview of the Balfour Declaration and subsequently became the Kingdom of Jordan. The remainder of the Mandate west of the Jordan River continued to be administered by the British under the terms of the Mandate.

---

*See Ronald Saunders, *The High Walls Of Jerusalem* (New York: Holt, Rinehart and Winston, 1984), an interesting history of the Balfour Declaration and the birth of the British Mandate for Palestine.

29

In 1947 after almost three decades of strife between Arabs and Jews, the British relinquished its Mandate and turned the area over to the United Nations. A UN proposal for partition of Palestine into Jewish and Palestinian states with an international trusteeship for the city of Jerusalem failed and the state of Israel was created in 1948 through force of arms in a portion of what had been mandatory Palestine. The remaining territory—the West Bank and the Gaza Strip—was occupied by Jordan and Egypt respectively. In the 1967 War Israel captured those areas, which it continues to hold. (The Golan Heights was also captured from Syria.)* In 1948, some three quarter million Palestinians fled their homes in the areas which became Israel.[2] In 1967 an additional one quarter million fled the areas captured by Israel.[3]

With the establishment of the State of Israel in 1948, it was the hope of the Jewish people that their dream of a peaceful homeland excelling as a "light unto nations" would finally be realized. Instead, Israel was engaged in wars in 1956, 1967, 1973 and 1982, and has experienced severe tension in the intervening periods.

Americans fully appreciate the Jewish longing for a return to the land of their forefathers and the establishment of a Jewish state. They are also committed to the absolute security of Israel. This support for Israel finds its basis in the accomplishments of the Jewish people, their contribution to Western culture, the history of anti-Semitism, and the unspeakable experience of the Holocaust.

While Americans are uniformly impatient with the failure of the Palestinians and the Arab states to recognize and accept Israel, many are also not well informed on Middle Eastern perceptions of the conflict. This has weighed heavily upon American policy. We may not, for example, be familiar with the Palestinian view that Palestine was not for the British or others to give away. They assert that Jews constituted 10 to 13 percent of the population of the Palestine Mandate in 1922[4] and 31 percent in 1946, shortly before Israel was created,[5] and that Jewish landholdings in 1947 are estimated to have constituted only 7 percent of the total land surface of Palestine, or 10 to 12 percent of its cultivable land.[6]

Palestinians assert that they had the same right of self-determination and independence as the British accorded Egypt, Iraq, and Transjordan. In response to the argument that they should have accepted the 1947 partition plan, Palestinians have pointed out that the Jewish state called for by the plan covered 55 percent of the contested land, includ-

---

*For additional historical background, see statement of The Legal Adviser, Department of State, April 21, 1978. Appendix A.

ing the richest farm land, and numbered as many Arab residents as Jewish.[7]

When land was acquired by the Jewish National Fund during mandatory times, it was "extra-territorialized"—held in trust by the Fund as the inalienable property of the Jewish people on which only Jewish labor could be employed.[8] Palestinians saw this as the transfer of their country to other hands.

Israel and its supporters today question whether Palestinians who seek a Palestinian state in the West Bank and the Gaza Strip would content themselves with those areas. Conversely, Palestinians, viewing partition as a possible Zionist stepping stone to a "Greater Israel",[9] have been skeptical of Israel's willingness to share the contested land.

Despite these tensions, it is the unanimous opinion of all concerned with a peaceful resolution of the conflict that partition is the only solution. Leonard Fein, editor and publisher of *Moment*, a magazine devoted to Jewish affairs, speaks for an increasingly large number of American Jews when he asserts that:

> it is fantasy to suppose that there can be both extended boundaries *and* peace. There may not be much chance for peace with partition, but there's no chance at all without it.[10]

Israel, today, thus faces a crisis. Will the West Bank and the Gaza Strip, together with their 1.3 million Palestinian inhabitants, be incorporated within the State of Israel? Or will these territories become a recognized homeland for their Palestinian inhabitants and for the three million other Palestinians in exile. How this issue is resolved could determine whether there will be future Arab-Israeli wars and whether American interests in a peaceful, stable Middle East can be furthered.

FOOTNOTES

1   Article 22, *Covenant of the League of Nations*, June 28, 1919. John Norton Moore, ed., *The Arab-Israeli Conflict* (Princeton: Princeton University Press, 1977), p. 888.

2   Moore, *The Arab-Israeli Conflict, supra*, p. xxiv, citing L. Holborn, "The Palestine Arab Refugee Problem," 23 *International Journal* 82, 88, 1968.

3   *Ibid.*, p. xxv.

4   *Ibid.*, p. xxi.

5   Ann Lesch, "Palestine: Land And People," in Nasser H. Aruri, ed., *Occupation: Israel Over Palestine*, Association Of Arab-American University Graduates, Inc., Belmont, Mass. 1983, p. 41.

6   *Ibid.*, p. 42.

7   *Ibid.*, p. 41.

8   *Ibid.*, p. 42.

9   Simha Flapan, *Zionism And The Palestinians*, (New York: Barnes and Noble, 1979). Ben-Gurion: "this is only a stage in the realization of Zionism;" Dr. Chaim Weizmann: "in the course of time we shall expand to the whole country. . . . this is only an arrangement for the next 25-30 years;" p. 257. Ben-Gurion: "after we become a strong force, as a result of the creation of a state, we shall abolish partition and expand to the whole of Palestine." p. 265.

10 Leonard Fein, "What, Then, Shall We Do?," *Moment*, April 1983.

II. *United Nations Security Council Resolution 242*

THE CAPTURE OF THE WEST BANK AND THE GAZA STRIP by Israel in the 1967 war produced United Nations Security Council Resolution 242 (Resolution 242)* and the principle of relinquishment of territories conquered by Israel in that war in exchange for Arab recognition and peace. Accepted by the U.S., Israel, and the international community, Resolution 242 emphasized "the inadmissibility of the acquisition of territory by war and the need to work for a just and lasting peace in which every State in the area can live in security."

Resolution 242 also affirmed that the establishment of such a peace should include "withdrawal of Israeli armed forces from territories occupied in the recent conflict" and the acknowledgement of the right of every state in the area "to live in peace within secure and recognized boundaries free from threats or acts of force." Arab governments attach importance to the fact that they have accepted Resolution 242. They consider their action should be recognized as their acceptance of Israel and as a reversal of their pre-1967 position.

In both the "Preamble" and "Framework" of the *Camp David Accords* of September 1978, it is stated that Resolution 242 "in all its parts" shall be the basis for peaceful settlement.[1] Despite these provisions, the Israeli governments of Menachem Begin and his successor, Yitzak Shamir, do not accept Resolution 242. Israel has not formally annexed the West Bank and the Gaza Strip. "You do not annex your own land," Prime Minister Begin explained. "This is the land of our forefathers. You annex foreign land."[2] His government asserted, furthermore, that the territories will never be relinquished, and his successor has echoed that determination. The "sacred work" of Jewish settlement "will continue unabated," Prime Minister Shamir has been quoted saying.[3] "We cannot postpone any advance in the settlement enterprise."[4]

---

*   See Appendix B.

1   *The Camp David Summit, September 1978*, Department of State Publication 8954, Near East and South Asian Series 88 (Washington, D.C.: USGPO, 1978). Resolution 242 was an annex to the agreements.

2   "Israel and the Palestinians, Will Reason Prevail?" TV documentary, produced by John Wallach, January 1981.

3   *The Washington Post*, October 11, 1983.

4   *The Jerusalem Post* (International Edition), December 18-24, 1983.

III. *Israel's West Bank Settlement Policy*

AFTER IT CONQUERED THE WEST BANK in 1967, Israel initially concentrated on building settlements in the Jordan Valley. Thereafter, Israelis who believed Israel has a religious and historical right to the West Bank—they use the Biblical names Judea and Samaria—forced the government to expand the areas of settlement. In 1970 the government approved the settlement of Kiryat Arba on the outskirts of Hebron, the West Bank's second largest city (and subsequently the scene of some of the West Bank's worst violence).

When the Begin government came to power in 1977, there were some 5,000 settlers in thirty-six settlements. The program of the Gush Emunim to settle all of *Eretz Yisrael* was then emphasized. With the Camp David Accords of 1978, President Carter considered there was an agreement to suspend further settlement activity, but Begin disagreed.

Mattityahu Drobles, Chairman of the World Zionist Federation's Settlement Division, whose planning guided government policy, described the strategy adopted after Camp David:

> In light of the current negotiations on the future of Judea and Samaria, it will now become necessary for us to conduct a race against time. During this period, everything will be mainly determined by the facts we establish in these territories and less by any other considerations. This is therefore the best time for launching an extensive and comprehensive settlement momentum, . . .[1]

When it became apparent that "there was no chance of populating the West Bank by ideology alone,"[2] the government resorted to massive subsidies. Land was given to developers at nominal cost. Buyers were given interest-free, non-indexed loans and outright grants. Israelis in effect were "bribed"[3] to settle by offers of housing at a fraction of its cost in Israel. Land expropriation was expanded. An old Turkish Land Code provision, for example, was used to claim uninhabited lands lying beyond the sound of human voice from the nearest village.[4] The burden of proof of ownership required of the Palestinians to offset such claims (they were given 21 days to produce full documentation of ownership), even if they and their forebears had worked the land for centuries, was almost impossible to satisfy.

Meron Benvenisti, a demographer and former Deputy Mayor of Jerusalem, concluded in a 1982 report:

> [I]t is clear that . . . there are no more limitations of land availability in the West Bank for Jewish settlements. . . .
>
> The combination of land acquisition, closure of areas for military purposes and land use planning, roads and intra-structure development, has already ensured complete Israel control over space in the West Bank.[5]

President Reagan called for a settlement freeze in conjunction with his September 1982 Plan. "[F]urther settlement activity is in no way necessary for the security of Israel," the President said. Begin's response—a conspicuous new drive—brought despair to his critics.

"These days," observed Leonard Fein, "it takes ideology to stay out of the West Bank, not to move into it."[6]   Another described the program as spelling "conquest, take-over, formal or tacit annexation."[7] "The subsidy is so heavy and massive," commented an Israeli, "only fools will not build their new homes here." Peace Now, Israel's best known coalition of peace activists, summarized these sentiments:

> —The expropriation of land on the West Bank constitutes an abuse of the principles of both Israeli and international law. Despite the legal fiction which formally authorizes these activities, they are essentially unjust. Through the implementation of an anachronistic law designed in other times and under different social realities, a situation has developed whereby an Arab family that has cultivated a plot of land for generations—in some cases for hundreds of years—is unable to prove ownership of its land.
>
> —It is universally recognized that land, in addition to being an important source of income, holds deep meaning for those who work it. The continuous assault on family homesteads, held for many generations, foments a deep-seated bitterness and hatred toward Israel, and therefore deepens the crisis between Israel and the Arabs.[8]

The costs of settlement have been difficult to determine. Its components are hidden within the budgets of several ministries. Peace Now has estimated the cost of settling a family on the West Bank at between $120,000 and $150,000.[9] It further estimates the cost of settling 100,000 Israelis on the West Bank (the 1986 goal of the Drobles plan) at $3 billion.[10] (The estimate of Hirsch Goodman, Defence Correspondent of *The Jerusalem Post*, is $1.5 billion to $4.5 billion.)[11] Still another Israeli analyst states that the settlement budget for 1983-84 calls for an annual expenditure of $470 million, exclusive of $80 to $100 million of subsidies to settlers.[12] The current Prime Minister, Yitzak Shamir, declares that these estimates are exaggerated, but he offers no evidence to refute them.[13] In early 1984 Finance Minister Cohen-Orgad is reported advising the Knesset that settlement costs were currently $400 million annually.[14]

ISRAELI SETTLEMENTS UNDER INTERNATIONAL LAW

HAGUE CONVENTION OF 1907:

"... Private property cannot be confiscated." Article 46

"The occupying state shall be regarded solely as administrator ... of real estate ... situated in the occupied country. ..." Article 55

"The property of municipalities, ... even when state property, shall be treated as private property. ..." Article 56

(The Annexed Regulations of the Hague Convention IV on the Laws and Customs of War on Land, 1907)

The position of the U.S. government is that the convention is applicable to the occupied territories.* Israel's High Court of Justice has ruled unanimously that it is applicable to the West Bank, that Israel's status there is that of a belligerent occupier with limited and temporary rights, and that "permanent" settlements are prohibited.**

FOURTH GENEVA CONVENTION:

"Protected persons who are in occupied territory shall not be deprived ... of the benefits of the present convention by any change introduced, as the result of the occupation of a territory, into the institutions or government of the said territory ... nor by any annexation ... of the occupied territory." Article 47

"Individual or mass forcible transfers, as well as deportations of protected persons from occupied territory to the territory of the Occupying Power or to that of any other country, occupied or not, are prohibited, regardless of their motive. Article 49(1)

"The Occupying Power shall not deport or transfer parts of its own civilian population into the territory it occupies." Article 49(6)

"Any destruction by the Occupying Power of real or personal property belonging individually or collectively to private persons, or the state ... is prohibited, except where such destruction is rendered absolutely necessary by military operation." Article 53

(The Geneva Convention/Relative to the Protection of Civilian Persons in Time of War, of August 12, 1949 [ratified by Israel on July 6, 1951])

The position of the U.S. government is that the convention is applicable to the occupied territories.† The Israeli High Court holds that it is enforceable only between countries that are parties to it and that individual inhabitants do not have standing to sue.††

---

*   See Statement of Ambassador Charles M. Lichenstein, Deputy United States Representative, to the United Nations Security Council, August 2, 1983. (Appendix C)

**   *Ayyub, et al. v. The Minister of Defence,* 1979, The High Court of Justice 606/78 610/78.

†   Statement of Ambassador Lichenstein, *supra.* "Israel, as the occupying power in the West Bank, is bound by the terms of the Fourth Geneva Convention."

††   *Ayyub, et al., supra.*

MAALE ADUMIM

The following is extracted from "The West Bank Story," *The B'nai B'rith International Jewish Monthly*, October 1983.

Maale Adumim is one of only a few West Bank communities established thus far where ideology has not been the main attraction. Rather, most of its residents were drawn by fantastic government housing subsidies . . .

The modern history of Maale Adumim, located just 15 miles from Jerusalem, began in 1974. In the wake of the Yom Kippur War, . . . the Gush Emunim (Block of the Faithful) movement sprang up, dedicated to settling the lands of Judea and Samaria. A religious group with a reputation for fanaticism, Gush Emunim gradually established settlements on the West Bank, often in defiance of the government. The settlements were populated by pioneering Orthodox Jews. . . .

At that time, Jews were forbidden to spend more than 48 hours on the West Bank, a law that sought to prevent illegal settlements from being founded. The workers at the Maale Adumim camp were supposed to live in nearby Jerusalem. But members of the Maale Adumim group squatted in the work camp. They hoped that their civilian presence would give them a foothold that would lead to a town. The government sent the army to evict them, but in April, the squatters returned, this time with a Sefer Torah. They designated a cement house in the camp as a synagogue, thereby safeguarding it from demolition by the government. Since a Torah was on the premises, a 24-hour guard was required. . . .

After various bureaucratic tussles with the government, the settlers were told that they could move 25 families to Maale Adumim to establish a legal settlement. . . .

In September 1982, shortly after President Ronald Reagan announced his Middle East peace plan calling for Israel to negotiate the future of the West Bank with Jordan and the Palestinians, the town of Maale Adumim was dedicated. Deputy Prime Minister David Levy spoke at the ceremony, directing his message to the new townspeople and across the desert and ocean to President Reagan: "Maale Adumim is here and will always be here." The Ashkenazic chief rabbi at the time, Shlomo Goren, quoted from the Talmud: "How do you acquire possession of Eretz Yisrael? By living in it." Journalists around the world called Maale Adumim the answer to the Reagan plan. . . .

By September 1983 the number of families on the West Bank has been estimated by Benvenisti at 6,500 (27,500 persons) and 200 in the Gaza Strip, and the total number of housing (family) units occupied, vacant, and under construction at 12,731.[15]

Zeev Ben Yosef, spokesman for the World Zionist Organization's Settlement Department, summed up the 1984 status of the program. "With the 114 settlements now existing, we can reach at least one million Jews" in the West Bank by the end of the century. His figures

WEST BANK 2,200 square miles (slightly larger than Delaware)
THE GAZA STRIP 145 square miles

JEWISH POPULATION IN THE WEST BANK
(not including the annexed "Greater Jerusalem")*

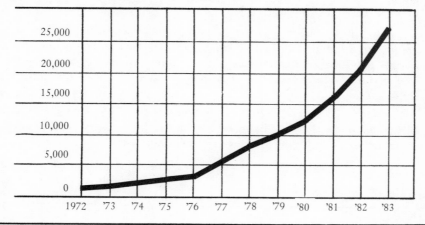

1983 POPULATION (estimated)

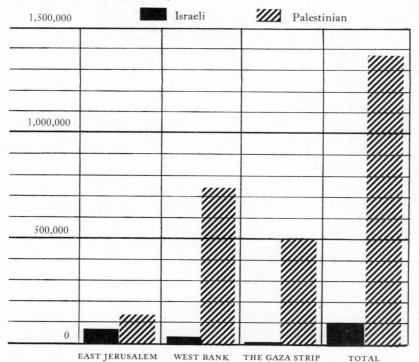

*Meron Benvenisti, *The West Bank Data Project,* American Enterprise Institute for Policy
Research, Washington, D.C., 1984, p.61.

THE BILLIONS GOING DOWN THE DRAIN

. . . What are we [Israel] investing yearly in the West Bank? There is no point in asking the [Israeli] Treasury—the government is guarding these data as a military secret. . . .

. . . there are no official figures: the government spends money; the Zionist organization spends money; the expenses are buried among a multitude of budget provisions so that neither you nor the inhabitants of Katamon [well-known slums of Jerusalem] will know how much is being invested in the West Bank. . . .

According to *The Jerusalem Post*, ten billion shekels [$200,000,000] a year are being invested in the West Bank, and as long as the Treasury does not publish other details we shall have to base ourselves on that estimate. . . .

AHARON GEVA, Israeli journalist
Davar, May 10, 1983

---

on housing units were substantially higher than those of Benvenisti. He stated that there were 7,000 units occupied, 6,000 others in the process of being occupied, and 12,000 under construction.[16]

"When inflation and the cost-of-living index are just historical memories," former Finance Minister Yoram Aridor has been quoted saying, "Judea and Samaria will be ours."[17]

FOOTNOTES

1   *Settlement In Judea And Samaria—Strategy, Policy And Plans,* Mattityahu Drobles, World Zionist Federation, Settlement Division, September 1980.
2   Hirsch Goodman, "Home Is Where The West Bank Is," *Sunday Times* [London], January 30, 1983.
3   David Richardson, "Settlements And Suburbia," *The Jerusalem Post* (International Edition), October 9-15, 1983.
4   Meron Benvenisti, *The West Bank And Gaza Data Base Project Pilot Study Report,* 1982, p. 32.
5   *Ibid.,* pp. 35, 38.
6   Fein, "What, Then Shall We Do?," *supra.*
7   Irving Howe, "The West Bank Trap," *The New Republic,* April 7, 1983.
8   *Everything You Didn't Want To Know About Settlement On The West Bank,* Peace Now Educational Activities, Jerusalem, 1983.
9   *Ibid.*
10 *Ibid.*
11 Goodman, "Home Is Where The West Bank Is," *supra.*
12 Israel Tomer, "Investment In The Territories," *Yediot Aharonot,* November 9, 1983.
13 *The Washington Post,* October 11, 1983.
14 "Testimony before Foreign Affairs Subcommittee," House of Representatives, Russell Misheloff, Director, Office of European Affairs, Bureau for Near East, Agency for International Development, February 1, 1984.
15 Benvenisti, *The West Bank Data Project, supra,* p.49.
16 *The New York Times,* February 12, 1984.
17 Christopher Walker, "Israel's Other Crisis," *The Spectator,* August 17, 1983.

HEBRON & ENVIRONS

Sea of Galilee

Mediterranean Sea

JORDAN

Jenin

Elon
Moreh
Hamra

Farah
Valley

Nablus

Mount Gerizim

Akraba

Gittit

JORDAN VALLEY

Jordan River

WEST BANK

Tel-Aviv

Ofra

Ain Yabrud
Beit El

Ramallah
El Bireh
Kalandia

Hadasha

Givon

Jericho

Jerusalem

Ma'ale
Adumim

ISRAEL

Gilo
Bethlehem

Efrat

Dead Sea

Halhoul

Hebron
Kiryat Arba

☆ Israeli Settlement

iles 5 4 3 2 1 0   5

Dahariya

"If we were to hear that some people in Holland were eager to incorporate 4 million Germans into their country against their will, we would conclude not that the proposers of that idea were patriots, but that they were demented. Yet the idea that Israel can permanently impose its authority over a foreign population which constitutes 30 percent of its own size is solemnly put forward as if it were a rational alternative.

"There does not exist on the face of the earth a single democratic country that would resemble what Israel would look like if it were permanently to control a foreign nation with a sharply defined personality, recognized as such by the entire world. . . ."

ABBA EBAN, former Foreign Minister of Israel
The Jerusalem Post, May 13, 1983

Hebron is a conservative Moslem city of 70,000, the second largest on the West Bank. The cave of Machpelah, under the Ibrahimi Mosque, in the center of the city, is holy to both Arabs and Jews as the burial place of Abraham.

"For the past fifteen years Hebron has been the linchpin of Israeli policy in the occupied territories. That was where the first struggle for settlement took place; it was from there that Gush Emunim's triumphal progress began, and from there that Gush Emunim contrived to get the better of the Israeli government. Kiryat Arba, Mearat Hamachpela, the Hadassah building, the House of Romano, and now the bus station — these are milestones in the achievement of Rabbi Levinger, whose beliefs and policy now virtually represent the official policy of the government of Israel. . . . Thus, slowly, but surely, the true struggle in the West Bank will become that for the expulsion of the Arabs."

DANI RUBINSTEIN, Israeli journalist
"The Fight For Expulsion," *Davar,* July 27, 1983

The settlement of Kiryat Arba, overlooking Hebron. In 1968 Gush Emunim activists sat in in downtown Hebron in defiance of Israeli government policy. They were given permission to move into a military base on the outskirts of the city. In 1970 this base was legalized as a regular civilian settlement and its borders expanded. Meron Benvenisti writes of "the existing tension in the Hebron area, where a community of Israeli zealots (Kiryat Arba) numbering 3,500 persons terrorizes and controls a population of 70,000 Palestinians."[1]

"Let us be clear. Jews have an historic right to live in Hebron, where Father Abraham is said, authoritatively, to be buried. Jews have a moral right to live wherever they please. But intelligence suggests that rights be exercised with decency and common sense, which means at times to restrain their exercise. If these settlers had come to Hebron saying they wished to live peacefully with the Arabs under whichever national authority prevailed, then no one could legitimately object to their presence. But they have not come to coexist. They have come to dominate, they have come to rule."

IRVING HOWE, author, historian
"The West Bank Trap," *The New Republic*, April 7, 1983

Since 1980 there has been a determined effort by settlers to restore the ancient Jewish quarter, which lies in the heart of Hebron's business and market district, and include the municipal fruit and vegetable market (above). Israeli sentry is in background.

"The time is not mature for Jewish owners to live in the middle of Hebron. Once we prepare the ground for it, everyone can live. . . . I'll take an Israeli passport and abide by Israeli laws, and you'll take an Arab passport and abide by their regulations."

MOHAMMED MILHEM, deported Mayor, Halhoul, West Bank
Speaking to an Israeli audience in West Jerusalem prior to
his deportation in May, 1980.

Israeli sentry above Hebron municipal fruit and vegetable market.

The settlers intend to link three formerly Jewish-owned buildings and build a complex of twenty-one apartments in the area of the market. Deputy Prime Minister David Levy envisions that the program will bring 500 families to the complex in the next three years.[2]

"Perhaps the worst sign" that "an ill wind is blowing against the direction of the Zionist vision, is that it is becoming hard to distinguish between the lunatic fringe and the mainstream of our political life. . . ."

AMNON RUBINSTEIN, Knesset Member and former Dean, Tel Aviv University Law School
Ha'aretz, March 19, 1982

In April 1983 settlers took over the municipal bus station (above) in the center of Hebron, claiming it to be Jewish property. The bus entrances were closed with barricades. Two thousand Peace Now members demonstrated in Hebron against the rebuilding project and for the return of the bus station to the municipality.

"The policies of the present government work systematically to create a version of Northern Ireland on the West Bank. . . . If Hebron becomes a new Belfast, can Jerusalem be far behind?"

MICHAEL WALZER, educator,
Institute for Advanced Study, Princeton, New Jersey
"Notes From An Israel Journal," *The New Republic,* September 5, 1983

Adjacent to the bus terminal is Beit Romano. A formerly Jewish-owned building which served as an Arab girl's school, Beit Romano was seized by the Army in 1982 for "military purposes" and then turned over to settlers. There are currently less than 100 Israelis in downtown Hebron.

"Walking through Hebron, I felt that I was encountering some profound malformation in Jewish life. In the center of the town several score Jewish settlers have planted themselves in an old, cramped Jewish quarter (Jews were driven out in the late 1920s after a bloody Arab pogrom.) Zealots who make nationalism into a pseudo religion and religion into ultranationalism, these settlers believe the Bible grants them unconditional sovereignty over this land. They are guarded by Israeli soldiers perched on rooftops and stationed in front of the Cave of Patriarchs, sacred to both Jews and Moslems."

IRVING HOWE, author, historian
"The West Bank Trap," *The New Republic*, April 7, 1983

*Israeli sentry in downtown Hebron. The influence of the Gush Emunim
on Israeli policy in the occupied territories has been substantial. "To tell the
truth," says a Gush Eminim settler from nearby Kiryat Arba, "we want them
to leave. And if they stay, they have to accept that this is a Jewish country,
not an Arab one. They will have to accept being ruled by us."*[3]

"To justify the settlements on the West Bank, [the government] argues that if these are not accepted, the heartland of historical Eretz Yisrael will become the only place on earth from which Jews are banned. It is false, because nowhere in the world can Jews settle *by force,* and because, if peace comes one day, there will be no reason why Jews, who for religious reasons want to live in Hebron, will necessarily be barred from doing so. It is false also because the aim is not so much to settle Israelis on that land as to deny it to the Palestinians."

MEIR MERHAV, Economics Editor, *The Jerusalem Post*
"Holy Egotism," *The Jerusalem Post* (International Edition),
July 8-14, 1979

*Change of Israeli patrol at Municipal Building, Hebron (October 1983).
In 1982 the Israeli High Court enjoined further building demolition by
settlers in downtown Hebron. In July 1983 Palestinian Mayor Mustapha
Natshe was dismissed and an Israeli, Zamir Shemesh, was appointed by the
occupation authorities. Among the reasons given for Natshe's dismissal
was that he had brought the lawsuit against the settlers. Mr. Shemesh,
following his appointment, caused the suit to be withdrawn.*

"Hebron is about an hour from Jerusalem, and along the way we saw Arab villages upon which the occupying authority had clamped a curfew. This is 'punishment' for the throwing of stones by Arab youths at passing Israeli vehicles. It's an eerie feeling: you ride through a village where every door is shut, every window-blind drawn, and some houses are marked with ominous Xs. What does this remind you of?"

IRVING HOWE, author, historian
"The West Bank Trap," *The New Republic*, April 7, 1983

Protest strikes by Palestinian merchants are prohibited. If merchants attempt to close their shops, the shops are either forced open, welded shut, or marked with a X or O for subsequent punishment.

A stone was thrown at an Israeli water truck in downtown Hebron in early June 1983. All shops were closed for one week. Twenty-four were welded shut. The shop pictured here, marked with O's, has not reopened.

"They [Mr. Milhem and Mr. Kawasmeh] told whoever was willing to listen that they are prepared for a full peace with Israel, but in their own independent state. . . . We were wrong in expelling two of the most outstanding and serious of the new leaders."

AMOS ELON, Israeli journalist;
author of "The Israelis, Founders and Sons"
Ha'aretz, June 1980

Palestinian farm lands between Hebron and nearby Halhoul. Halhoul Mayor Mohammed Milhem, who openly advocated Palestinian peace with Israel, was deported in May, 1980. The United Nations Security Council in December 1980 voted unanimously that he and Fahd Kawasmeh, the Hebron mayor deported with him, be permitted to return to their homes. The resolution has been disregarded by Israel.

"[W]hat kind of a Jewish state shall we have in another ten, twenty years if Israel takes upon itself the permanent control and repression of another million Arabs? Is there any reason to suppose that the Palestinians will become a docile, law-abiding minority, willing and content to live under Israeli rule? What will be the effect of continuing military repression of Palestinian violence on Israeli society? It is assumed that a nation can engage in such domination year after year and somehow remain immune to the insidious effects, morally speaking, of occupation."

HENRY SIEGMAN, Executive Director, American Jewish Congress
Ha'aretz, March 9, 1983

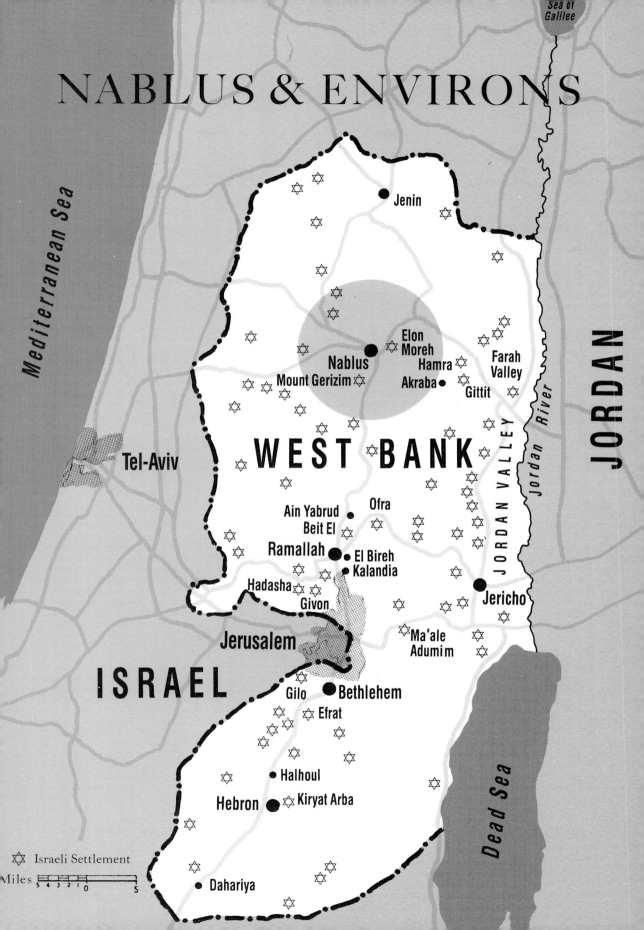

NABLUS & ENVIRONS

Sea of Galilee

Mediterranean Sea

JORDAN

Jenin

Elon Moreh

Nablus
Mount Gerizim

Hamra
Akraba

Farah Valley

Gittit

WEST BANK

JORDAN VALLEY

Jordan River

Tel-Aviv

Ain Yabrud
Beit El

Ofra

Ramallah
El Bireh
Kalandia

Hadasha

Givon

Jericho

Jerusalem

Ma'ale Adumim

ISRAEL

Gilo
Bethlehem

Efrat

Halhoul

Hebron
Kiryat Arba

Dead Sea

Dahariya

✡ Israeli Settlement

Miles 5 4 3 2 1 0   5

"The name of our sickness is the Palestinian problem. As long as we are locked into a hostility which leads to a war every five or ten years, there is no hope that our society can change for the better. The only way out is to strike a compromise with the Palestinians and with the rest of the Arabs, based on two elements: security for Israel and self-determination for the Palestinians. Self-determination was the flag we waved decades ago when we demanded our own state. How can we now deny it to others?"

ZVI KESSE, Israeli educator and sociologist
Interview, *Newsweek*, February 21, 1983

Downtown Nablus. Its 90,000 Palestinian residents make it the largest city on the West Bank. Settlers are now determined to establish a permanent Jewish presence in the heart of the city.

"There is nothing more contemptible and harmful than the use of religious sanctions in a conflict between nations. It is doubtful whether the young man from Gush Emunim who made the Elon Moreh appeal had any idea of the Pandora's box he was opening. . . .

"A religious claim is valid when it relates to matters between people and their creator—to prayer, fast, atonement, faith, and ritual. It does, however, inspire opposition if it disregards others' claims and assumes the right to impose its way, or to harm the rights, freedoms, and interests of others. A religious claim will give a strong impression of hubris, an ambition of mastery, if it tries to subordinate the believers of one religion to those of another. It is one thing for the believer to remain within the boundaries of debate over passages in his holy books and theological commentaries; it is quite another if behind him stands tanks, planes, missiles, soldiers, and police, ready to use direct or indirect violence."

J. L. TALMON, Israeli historian
"The Homeland Is In Danger," *Dissent*, Fall 1980

(Photo: SIGMA)

Gush Emunim settlers pray at the first site of Elon Moreh, above Nablus, the morning after the settlement was established (June 8, 1979). The Israeli High Court of Justice ruled unanimously that the "security" arguments of the government disguised its true political intentions, and that the settlement had to be dismantled. When the settlement was moved to a nearby site, the Palestinians whose land was taken were unable to satisfy the severe standard of proof required by the authorities for ownership of land.

"Despite having occupied the West Bank for fifteen years, the Israelis can enter that territory only on armed patrol. . . . What kind of normality can there be when 3,500,000 Jews are prepared to turn nearly 2,000,000 Palestinians into second-class citizens, with all the cultural, social, and economic degradation this means?"

JACOBO TIMERMAN, journalist and author
The Longest War, New York: Alfred A. Knopf, 1982, p. 32

Israeli Defense Forces on patrol in Nablus (April, 1982).

"Standing here among the piles of barbed wire and shooting posts above Nablus, spread out over the steep slopes of the mountainside, one can only marvel at the impulsion that is now driving us to thrust ourselves into this area—clumsy, self-satisfied, arrogant and power-drunk, into the dense Arab populations whose basic civil rights we are trampling underfoot and whose land, private and public, we are taking away from them."

> AMOS ELON, Israeli journalist and author
> "A View From Mount Gerizim," *Ha'aretz*, February 4, 1983

"It must be recalled that the settlements do not add Jews—they simply disperse them. They do not reduce the Arab population; they simply provoke it. In fact, the settlements are adding Arabs to the future State of Israel. For when we settle on Mount Bracha, we are not adding 1,000 Jews to the State of Israel; rather, we are adding 400,000 Arabs living in the Nablus area to the rich fabric of the State of Israel. We are extending Israeli rule over a relatively small area, and arousing a relatively large population against us. We shall create a demographic melange which will prove impossible to correct in the future, and we will create a growing security problem that will place a heavier burden on the shoulders of the state. While we can make an omelette out of eggs, we cannot make eggs out of an omelette."

> AMNON RUBINSTEIN, Knesset Member and former Dean, Tel Aviv University Law School
> *Ha'aretz*, May 10, 1983

Construction commences at Bracha settlement on Mount Gerizim, overlooking Nablus (July 1983). Nearly 1,000 acres of land on adjoining hilltops have been confiscated for Bracha "B" and Bracha "C". Ariel Sharon, when Defense Minister, said the area would become "the Kiryat Arba" of Nablus.[4]

"The illusion that peace will come about in the Middle East without sacrifice is self-defeating. Our enemies will not suddenly disappear. There is no reason to think that three million Jews can live among 120,000,000 Arabs without a political settlement."

EDGAR BRONFMAN, President, World Jewish Congress
Biannual Meeting, Washington, D.C.,
reported by Zeev Barak, *Yediot Aharonot,* February 2, 1983

"In the long run, no American government can accept the annexation of the West Bank and Gaza because such a measure would mean that the Palestinian problem is insoluble."

RABBI ARTHUR HERTZBERG, former President,
American Jewish Congress
"Vanishing Jews," interview by David Krivine, *The Jerusalem Post* (International Edition), December 11-17, 1983

Abu Jish standing in front of fields in the fertile Farah Valley east of Nablus that were taken from him in 1970 for the settlement of Hamra. (His old irrigation system is in the foreground.) Since 1978 the occupation authorities have disapproved a United States-funded feasibility study for a project to upgrade an open irrigation canal used by Farah Valley Palestinians since the 1930's. The project would involve no new water. It would only conserve water already in use. No part of the cost of the ultimate project would be borne by the Israeli government.

"Most of our people either oppose or have strong reservations about the settlements. Needless to say, world public opinion universally denounces the current policy as a violation of international law and, indeed, as a unilateral provocation that makes the idea of negotiation seem ridiculous. From this follows the conspiratorial pattern in which these settlements are established, and the way they are fenced in, 'for military purposes.' The seizure or purchase of land, 'for public use,' proceeds much in the same way. This is not the way a sovereign, law-abiding nation should operate, nor is it the way of a society whose openness, until now, has always been one of its most admirable qualities."

J. L. TALMON, Israeli historian
"The Homeland Is In Danger," *Dissent,* Fall 1980

Fields once cultivated by Palestinians from the village of Akraba, 10 miles southeast of Nablus. They are part of 1,250 acres of farmland closed by the Israeli Defense Forces in 1971 for "military training purposes". In early 1972 the IDF sprayed wheat fields of Akraba farmers which lay inside the closed areas with chemical defoliants. The fields are now farmed by Israeli settlers from Gittit.

"Let a researcher in Political Science point to one country except Israel whose foreign policy is based on a principle that the whole world rejects, namely that the territories conquered in '67 are an integral part of Israel."

ABBA EBAN, former Foreign Minister of Israel
Interview by Yaron London, *Ha'ir,* September 23, 1983

JORDAN VALLEY
EAST OF NABLUS

Sea of Galilee

Mediterranean Sea

JORDAN

Jordan River

JORDAN VALLEY

Jenin

Elon
Moreh
Hamra
Akraba
Gittit

Farah
Valley

Nablus
Mount Gerizim

WEST BANK

Tel-Aviv

Ofra
Ain Yabrud
Beit El
Ramallah
El Bireh
Kalandia
Hadasha
Givon
Jericho

Ma'ale
Adumim

Jerusalem

ISRAEL

Gilo
Bethlehem
Efrat

Dead Sea

Halhoul

Hebron
Kiryat Arba

✡ Israeli Settlement

Miles 5 4 3 2 1 0   5

Dahariya

"People say that Jordan is Palestine, that a majority of the Jordanian population is Palestinian. But that's true because there are so many refugees in Jordan. To use that as an argument is to raise the question, *haratzachtah v'gam yarashtah?*—you've killed, and now you propose to inherit? . . ."

MERON BENVENISTI, former Deputy Mayor of Jerusalem quoted in Leonard Fein, "What, Then, Shall We Do?," *Moment,* April 1983

Farm lands of Gittit settlement. During severe 1979 drought, no water was allocated to nearby Auja farmers, except a one-inch pipe for drinking water, while swimming pools at Gittit continued to operate. Since the military occupation began in 1967, with but a few exceptions Palestinians have been permitted to drill no wells for irrigation. The estimated Jordan Valley settler population is 700 families.

"The moral catastrophe of the West Bank will have every appearance, initially, of a political success. The Israelis will rule over the Arabs with imperial benevolence, though if there is much resistance, with a hard fist. The United States will provide the money for a policy it says it dislikes. The American Jewish leaders will moan privately and applaud publicly. The United Jewish Appeal will send delegations that will report home 'with pride' on the new towns in the West Bank. And some people—who can say how many?—will be saddened by the thought that a Jewish state which had begun with such splendid reserves of social idealism should now, at least in part, rest on a structure of injustice."

IRVING HOWE, author, historian
"The West Bank Trap," *The New Republic,* April 7, 1983

RAMALLAH & ENVIRONS

Sea of Galilee

Mediterranean Sea

JORDAN

Jenin

Elon Moreh
Nablus
Mount Gerizim
Hamra
Akraba
Farah Valley
Gittit

WEST BANK

Tel-Aviv

JORDAN VALLEY

Jordan River

Ain Yabrud
Ofra
Beit El
Ramallah
El Bireh
Kalandia

Hadasha
Givon

Jericho

Jerusalem

Ma'ale Adumim

ISRAEL

Gilo
Bethlehem
Efrat

Halhoul

Hebron
Kiryat Arba

Dead Sea

✡ Israeli Settlement

Miles 5 4 3 2 1 0   5

Dahariya

"Mr. Begin and his colleagues have their own way with language and believe they can make words mean anything they want them to mean. When they speak of 'no preconditions,' they mean unconditional surrender; when they speak of 'autonomy,' they mean subjugation, and when they speak—as they so often do—of Jews and Arabs living together in peace, equality and friendship, they mean resignation to Jewish rule."

CHAIM BERMANT, journalist
The Jewish Chronicle, London, April 15, 1983

Israeli troops force open Palestinian shops in Ramallah during general strike called to protest removal of Ibrahim Tawil, mayor of nearby El Bireh (March 22, 1982). Authorities have removed the mayors of eight of the eleven largest West Bank cities elected in Israeli-supervised elections in 1976, the last elections held on the West Bank.

"An entire brand of Zionism has gone bankrupt. That same Zionism that has believed, since the era of Ben Gurion, that successful military might would exempt Israel from the need to give to the Palestinians a place in the Land of Israel that would allow them, too, to establish a state."

AMOS KENAN, Israeli journalist and writer
Yediot Aharonot, September 2, 1983

Ramallah shopkeeper asks Israeli Defense Forces officer why his shop is being forced open. (March 22, 1982)

"Israel is today the main military power in the Middle East, and is not facing any major threats to its security. . . . Israel's settlements policies and its current policies toward the Palestinians contradicts American Jewish values and American interests, and I believe they are also hurting Israeli interests."

RITA HAUSER, Chairman, Foreign Affairs Committee, American Jewish Committee
Interview by Leon Hadar, *The Jerusalem Post,* April 25, 1983

Israel Defense Forces patrol streets of Ramallah, March 25, 1982, in wake of demonstrations to protest removal of Ibrahim Tawil, mayor of neighboring El Bireh. Despite the intense Israeli settlement program of recent years, the 1,300,000 Palestinians who reside in the West Bank and the Gaza Strip constitute 97% of the population of these two areas.

"The next generation . . . may well ask where were we—Jewish citizens, members of the liberal professions, intellectuals, authors and artists? It will want to know why we ceased to protest when before our very eyes the new Israel was being formed. . . .

"They will ask: why were you silent when you saw political murder being committed, and a series of political crimes, mainly on the West Bank, remaining uninvestigated owing to the partiality of the Israeli authorities, who are afraid of the armed militias of Jews roving the hills of the area and taking the Lord's name in vain? . . .

"No one listened to us, that is all. And the deeper fear that gnawed away inside us was that even if the corrupting rule of the Likud were replaced by the Alignment, the Alignment could do nothing to deflect Israel and Zionism from the historic direction being mapped out by the zealots and the contractors. . . ."

EHUD BEN-EZER, Israeli journalist
"Were We Silent?" *Davar,* May 20, 1983

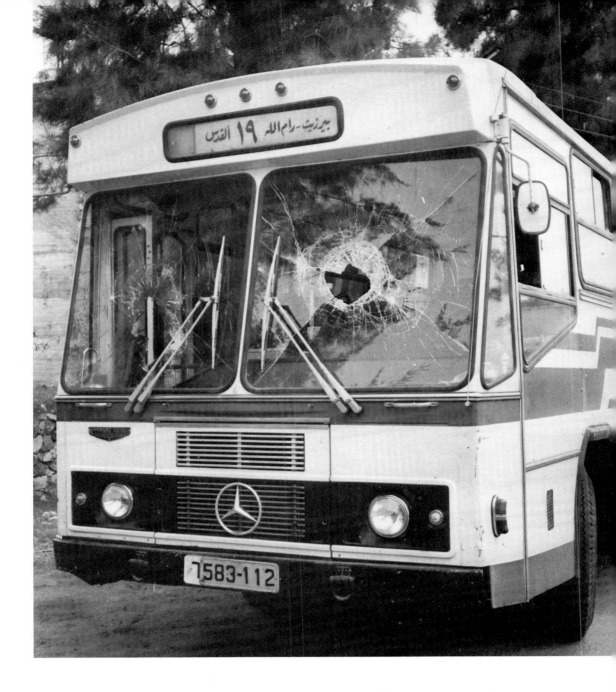

Early the morning of October 26, 1983, men "in uniform" used rifles to smash bus of the Bir Zeit Bus Company, at the home of manager Ibrahim Awadalla. A fire was started near its gas tank. Such vandalism and harassment of Palestinians are common-place.

Avraham Achitur, former Israeli intelligence chief, states that the settlements are a "psychological breeding ground for Jewish terror" and that Jewish terror "is now receiving strong backing from the government."[5]

"You stop the stones at Jalazoun only to be faced with rocks at Kalandia. When you use water cannon to subdue Kalandia, you face riots at Dahariya. You get things under control at Dahariya and tires are burned on the main road outside Deheisha."

The Jerusalem Post

*Occupation authorities have barricaded the main entrance to the Kalandia
neighborhood (between Ramallah and Jerusalem), home to 7,000 Palestinians.
(October, 1983)*

*When there are disturbances and disorder, curfews are imposed on Palestinian
communities, never on Israeli settlements. The recent human rights report
of the International Center for Peace in the Middle East, Tel Aviv, (the
HUMAN RIGHTS REPORT) observed that "continued rule has allowed Israel
to 'perfect' methods of punishment. . . . The outstanding characteristic is the
extensive, almost daily use of collective punishment."[6]*

"Public opinion in democratic countries has in the past been willing to take account of military factors justifying our occupation of the West Bank, and at times even to accept them. But they will no longer countenance nationalistic, mystical religious demands to establish our dominion over a million Arabs and appropriate their lands on the basis of 'rights' dating back three thousand years.

"The State is squandering tens of billions of shekels . . . at a time when there are no funds to heat schools and tens of thousands of elderly people are suffering from cold for lack of the means to heat their homes. Billions are being poured into the untillable lands of the West Bank while there is no money to maintain what we have in the Avara. [The plains of the Negev — Ed.]"

ELIAHU SALPETER, Israeli journalist
Ha'aretz, January 23, 1983

Saleh Hassounea struggles to hold his farm bordering the Beit-El settlement (background) near Ramallah. In litigation involving Palestinian lands taken for this settlement, the Israeli High Court of Justice ruled that the Hague Convention of 1907 is applicable to the West Bank, that Israel's status is that of a belligerent occupier with limited and temporary rights, and that "permanent" Israeli settlements are prohibited.[7]

"[D]issent must never be equated with disloyalty. . . .

"Must we indulge in annexationist fantasies in order to prove that we are passionate Jews? Must I justify every single restrictive measure in Judea and Samaria in order to demonstrate my love for Israel? Is that love diminished in the slightest when I assert that the incorporation of these territories into Israel represents a threat to the Jewish essence of the State?

"So let us once and for all reject the notion that by speaking the truth as we see it, by giving the Israelis our own perception of events, we are somehow treasonous. I believe instead that Israel is, indeed, the possession, the treasure and the burden of the entire Jewish people, and that gives us both the right and the responsibility to speak out. . . .

"[T]here are some issues that are so fundamental in determining the character of the Jewish people's future that we have to assert our views even at the risk of overstepping propriety. And the West Bank, it seems to me, is surely such an issue. It is not an operational detail; it goes to the very heart and nature of what the Jewish state is all about, and to be silent on such a fundamental issue would be a tragic mistake."

ALEXANDER SCHINDLER, President, Union of American Hebrew Congregations; former Chairman of the Conference of Presidents of Major Jewish Organizations "Truth-Telling And Leadership Responsibility In American Jewish Life," *Moment,* March 1983

The Hadasha settlement, six miles northwest of Jerusalem, founded in late 1979, includes land taken from the Sabri Gharib family (see photograph next page). The Gharibs struggle to hold their remaining land.

"We hold the [West Bank] as trustees only. It is elementary that a trustee who takes for himself from the trust property is stealing in one of the ugliest ways."

HAIM COHEN, Deputy President Emeritus,
Israel High Court of Justice

Sabri Gharib, whose wife is pictured here and whose family has been working their land for generations, recounts experiences common to West Bank farmers: the Israeli High Court of Justice has issued three different restraining orders intended to protect him and his family of eleven from settler harassment; in the two years 1981-1982, he and his family were beaten three times, arrested, jailed or detained eight times, twice had identity cards confiscated, received threats to demolish their home, and were harassed in other ways, including being fired upon. [8]

"Israelis . . . are . . . being rather disingenuous when they say that their only goal is to arrive at 'coexistence' or 'life together' with the Palestinians. Such a relationship is not necessarily egalitarian. Between a rider and his horse there is also coexistence. As long as Israel takes 'life together' to mean that it will be allowed to rule in the West Bank, this particular form of coexistence will surely prove unpalatable both to the Palestinian Arabs and to the world at large."

GENERAL YEHOSHAFAT HARKABI
former Chief of Israeli Military Intelligence
"Striving To Attain The Possible," *Can The Palestinian Problem Be Solved?*, The Van Leer Jerusalem Foundation, 1983

Ain Yabrud resident points to his fruit trees enclosed within the barbed-wire perimeter of the Ofra settlement, 12 miles north of Jerusalem. Ofra began as a "work camp" in early 1975 when Defense Minister Shimon Peres of the Labor Government authorized "overnight lodging" at a former Jordanian Army camp near Ain Yabrud. The Begin government subsequently allowed Gush Emunim settlers to expand Ofra on adjacent privately owned Palestinian land.

"Redemption of the land *(geulat haqarqa)* is a fundamental Zionist concept loaded with supreme symbolic and ideological significance. It is land that the Jewish people sought to liberate. The national conflict with the Palestinians was perceived as a conflict not between equal peoples but between one legitimate collective and a local population that happened to be squatting on that land. The history of the Zionist enterprise is an account of physical *faits accomplis* through land acquisition and settlement, created to achieve national, political, and military objectives. Most Israelis perceive the occupation of the territories as a direct continuation of the Zionist enterprise. The policies of 'land reclamation' are therefore vigorously pursued.

"The Palestinians, attaching the same macronational and symbolic value to the land, resist Israeli land acquisition efforts with whatever means they can muster. The unequal strength of the conflicting parties, however, dictates the results. The Israelis, backed by the full coercive power of a sovereign state and by vast material resources, succeed through a variety of methods in attaining their objectives and in gaining control over more and more areas."

MERON BENVENISTI, former Deputy Mayor of Jerusalem
The West Bank Data Project, supra, p. 19.

(Photo: Wide World)

Gush Emunim settlers erect fence around tent at Givon settlement, ten miles northwest of Jerusalem, on December 27, 1977. In 1978 the Begin government supported Givon, together with Ma'ale Adumim and Efrat, as an outer ring of large urban estates around Jerusalem. The total planned population of Givon is 30,000.

"In its 16th year the occupation looks more permanent than ever. Every passing day brings us nearer to an apartheid state. The only wonder is that many are still affronted, quite genuinely, when you say that. 'This is not apartheid, it is security,' they say, or, 'Let the Arabs agree to autonomy.' But people who speak this way have usually not troubled to read what we actually offered to the Arabs in the autonomy proposal—even less than the South Africans have accorded to their Bantustans. . . ."

AMOS ELON, Israelis journalist and writer
"Shame On The West Bank," *Dissent*, Spring 1983

BETHLEHEM & ENVIRONS

Sea of Galilee

Mediterranean Sea

JORDAN

Jenin

Elon Moreh
Hamra
Farah Valley

Nablus

Mount Gerizim
Akraba
Gittit

Jordan River

WEST BANK

JORDAN VALLEY

Ofra

Ain Yabrud
Beit El

Ramallah
El Bireh
Kalandia

Tel-Aviv

Hadasha
Givon

Jericho

Jerusalem

Ma'ale Adumim

ISRAEL

Gilo
Bethlehem
Efrat

Dead Sea

Halhoul

Hebron
Kiryat Arba

Dahariya

✡ Israeli Settlement

Miles 5 4 3 2 1 0   5

"[Zionism's] success, so vastly impressive and rapid, achieved in the span of a few decades, has in turn produced a wave of irrationality so powerful that it threatens to sweep aside all realism, all caution, all sober thought. The pendulum has swung fast and far toward messianism, eschatology, and chiliasm in their myriad manifestations, religious, quasi-religious, and secular. . . . It is touch and go whether Zionism can survive the effects of its own triumph. . . .

"For the most part . . . the Israeli leadership and people have found themselves increasingly unable to handle the problem of the territories conquered in 1967. . . .

"The 'primitivization' of political thinking . . . is not the product of the Begin years, even though the Likud has built on it, fosters it, and may well perpetuate it. . . .

"If Labor does come back to power . . . it should ensure before all else that it takes over the Ministry of Education. It is high time to weaken the hold of mysticism and myth. Labor is unlikely to have another chance."

JONATHAN FRANKEL, Professor of Russian and Jewish history,
Hebrew University of Jerusalem
"Bar Kochba and All That," *Dissent*, Spring 1984

Construction underway at the Efrat settlement, ten miles south of Jerusalem. Plans for Efrat were drawn up under the Labor Government in 1975. The Begin government launched Efrat in 1978 as one of three large settlements to ring Jerusalem. There is little contact between the West Bank settlers and Palestinian residents. Most settlements are surrounded by barbed wire. One half of West Bank settlers commute to work within Israel.

"Wherever they settle, the Jews carry the Israeli administrative, political, and welfare state system. They build their own high-level physical infrastructure and enjoy the generous subisidies that attracted them to the West Bank. Imbued with nationalistic pathos, they will monopolize the environment. The Arabs will remain subject to the norms of the military government, disfranchised and discriminated against even when officially annexed to Israel (like the East Jerusalem Palestinian community), excluded from the benefits of the Israeli welfare system even when they are full-time employees in Israeli enterprises, lacking proper physical infrastructure, fragmented and harassed, and powerless to shape their future or to resist further encroachment."

MERON BENVENISTI, former Deputy Mayor of Jerusalem
The West Bank Data Project, supra, p. 62

Mohammed Darwish and family work their tomato field beneath the Efrat settlement.(October 1983) Twenty dunams of their land were "closed" for "security" reasons in 1979 and subsequently used for the settlement. Darwish has been told by Efrat settlers that his remaining land "will, in time, be a playground for our school".

"Israel's unprecedented dependence on American aid partly derives, ironically, from the Begin government's extravagant investment in the West Bank. Israel is using about $200 million a year to build housing, shopping centers, and industry there. . . . Begin, to be blunt, is using American money to create a *fait accompli* that will make it impossible to carry out the American government's policy."

BERNARD AVISHAI, Assistant Professor of Writing,
Massachusetts Institute of Technology
"Can Begin Be Stopped?," *The New York Review of Books,* June 2, 1983

Gilo, the largest settlement in the occupied West Bank, as seen from near Bethlehem.

"[T]he time for business as usual is over. American Jews must play a loud, vocal role in opposing the policies of Begin and the World Zionist Organization. We must shout from the rooftops: *No more settlements!* . . . Anyone who cares about Israel's future must begin efforts to obstruct the settlement policy."

Editorial, *The Jewish Frontier*, New York, May 1983

The Gilo settlement, with home of Halima Abdul Nabi in foreground. Mrs. Nabi, a 70-year old Palestinian widow, once had a four-room home on a 12-dunam (three acre) fruit orchard. In 1970 her land was confiscated for "public purposes". In 1976, without notice, bulldozers uprooted her orchard, and settlement construction commenced. The pictured staircases went through her washroom and kitchen. Mrs. Nabi was imprisoned for three days for resisting the taking of her land. She is left with two rooms and one tree.

"There is not one precedent, from anywhere in the world, that permits us to think that the policies Israel now follows can have a happy ending, a pacific result. . . .

"I do not know how most American Jews react to these matters. It is my impression that a very large number have preferred not to acknowledge what is in fact taking place, because so much pain attends the acknowledgment. And I know, as well, that there are some in this community who welcome Israel's policies, who share the hysterical vision that gives them birth. But I strongly suspect that there are also very many American Jews who tremble for the fate of the Third Commonwealth. Some are disturbed by the ethical consequences of the present policies; most believe that those policies, for all the grandiose rhetoric by which they are defended, are a prescription for practical disaster."

LEONARD FEIN, educator, author
"American Jews And The West Bank," *Moment,* May 1982

The Tamerah family of Bethlehem (on the West Bank) views rubble of their dynamited home. On November 14, 1981, an Israeli bus was the subject of a fire bomb attack by youths on the highway passing through Bethlehem. There were no injuries. On November 16, 1981, sixteen-year-old Afiyeh Tamerah was arrested on suspicion of being an accomplice. Eighteen hours later the Israel Defense Forces demolished the newly finished home of the Tamerah family which housed Afiyed, his parents, and twelve relatives. THE JERUSALEM POST *reported that this and four other concurrent house demolitions were "a manifestation of [Defense Minister Ariel] Sharon's declared policy to clamp down heavily on residents opposed to the [Camp David] autonomy plan.*[9] *The* HUMAN RIGHTS REPORT *states that 34 homes were demolished in 1980-81, and 35 were demolished or sealed in 1982.*[10]

"This policy [of increasing settlements] is the major obstacle to any moderate Arab initiatives for a peaceful resolution of differences. Israel must halt its settlement policy—a move that alone might break the diplomatic logjam."

JIMMY CARTER and GERALD R. FORD

"A Time For Courage In The Middle East," *Reader's Digest*, February 1983

Ma'ale Adumim, on the road to Jericho, six miles east of Jerusalem (pictured here in December 1978). Ma'ale Adumim was founded by the Gush Emunim in 1974. To avoid eviction under a law forbidding Israelis to spend more than 48 hours on the West Bank, the settlers imported a Torah. A 24-hour guard was then necessary to protect the Torah.

"We reside and move freely all over Eretz Israel; they may not. They are confined to a 'pale of settlement' as the Jews of Czarist Russia once were and the blacks of South Africa are today. In exactly the same way, they may not work or remain outside their areas of residence. They are not allowed to buy property this side of the Green Line [i.e., inside the 1967 borders of Israel—Ed.], while we may buy anywhere we wish, and most of our purchases are made with generous assistance from the government. Land is expropriated from them to be given to us, but never the other way round. According to the official doctrine, public land should routinely serve our social aims, but never theirs."

AMOS ELON, Israeli journalist and writer
"Shame On The West Bank," *Dissent*, Spring 1983

Ma'ale Adumim, in September 1982, when it was dedicated as a planned community of 10,000 housing units. 1,500 families were attracted to Ma'ale Adumim in 1983. It has 18 kindergartens, 75 small factories, three synagogues.

By September 1983 the number of housing (family) units in all West Bank settlements (occupied, vacant, and under construction) was 12,427.[11] Israel's settlement budget exceeds that for education. Many Israelis are alarmed at the impact of settlement expenditures on both defense and social service needs.

"Shalom Tuitan is a mechanic by trade, but works as an odd-job man for a Jerusalem newspaper. He can barely make ends meet on a salary of around [$275] a month. But he is the proud owner of a spanking new, five-room double-storey villa, with a 282 square-metre garden [in Ma'ale Adumim].

"He received it almost as a gift from the government. Two-thirds of the cost was covered by an outright government grant; the remaining third, roughly [$6,000] is to be paid back in the form of an unlinked mortgage over 25 years.

"Not a bad deal in a country where the annual inflation rate is more than 130 percent. In 25 years, at the rate things are going in Israel, the [$6,000] should be worth a couple of shillings."

HIRSH GOODMAN, Defence Correspondent, *The Jerusalem Post*
"Home Is Where The West Bank Is," *Sunday Times* [London],
January 30, 1983

1983 advertisement in THE JERUSALEM POST. *Promoters place colorful double-page settlement advertisements extolling the spacious yards, beautiful scenery and all the advantages of suburbia. Unable to find a sufficient number of ideologically committed Israelis, the government now seeks to attract settlers with massive subsidies. The cost of Israel's settlement program is estimated at $300,000,000 annually.*

FOOTNOTES

1   Benvenisti, *The West Bank Data Project*, supra, p. 61.

2   Richard Bernstein, "Israelis Approve Ouster of Mayor in West Bank City," *The New York Times*, July 11, 1983.

3   Richard Bernstein, "Cycle of Vengeance Haunts Hebron's Recent History," *The New York Times*, September 12, 1983.

4   Amos Elon, "A View From Mount Gerizim," *Ha'aretz*, February 4, 1983.

5   *Ha'aretz*, August 22, 1983.

6   *Human Rights In The Occupied Territories 1979-1983* (Tel Aviv: International Center For Peace In The Middle East, November 1983), p. 168.

7   *Ayyub, et al., supra.*

8   *In Their Own Words*, Affidavits Collected by Law in the Service of Man, Ramallah, 1983, pp. 13-16.

9   *The Jerusalem Post* (International Edition), November 22-28, 1981.

10 *Human Rights, supra*, p. 157.

11 Benvenisti, *The West Bank Data Project, supra*, p. 49.

IV. *Conditions of West Bank Occupation*

THE FULL IMPLICATIONS of Israel's West Bank settlements can be understood only when viewed in the context of the government's general attitude toward the West Bank and Palestinians. "Non-recognition of Palestinians remains . . . the basic tenet of Israel's policymakers," writes Simha Flapan.[1] He further observed:

> The Zionist attitude towards the pan-Arab national movement has been the subject of many important studies. But little attention has been paid specifically to the Palestinian component of the problem. Even an excellent work such as Aharon Cohen's *Israel and the Arab World*, which describes in detail contacts between Arabs and Jews, subsumes the Palestinian-Zionist conflict within the framework of relations between Jews and the Arab national movement in general.[2]

The Labor government, before Begin, saw the solution in territorial compromise with Jordan. The rationale of the Begin and Shamir governments is less clear. They oppose relinquishing any portion of what they view as the land of "Greater Israel," and few observers believe that the terms of the autonomy which have been offered the Palestinians under the *Camp David Accords* merit serious consideration.

Israel's occupation of the West Bank is now in its seventeenth year. In 1983 former President Jimmy Carter observed:

> There's been a dramatic change in the last two years in land-taking by the Israeli government, and also a rapid deterioration in the life quality of Palestinians on the West Bank and Gaza. . . . This military occupation has gone on now for [sixteen years.]. And the deplorable conditions on the West Bank and Gaza among the Palestinians is [sic] not well known by the outside world.[3]

A recent report on human rights in the occupied territories from the International Center For Peace in the Middle East in Tel Aviv (the *Human Rights Report*), states:

> The ruling authorities have ignored the principles of international pacts concerning the rights of a civilian population in occupied territory, undermined people's freedom and their basic rights, used collective punishment and punishment of the surroundings, and transformed humiliation into a system of rule.[4]

121

Though the Geneva Convention grants an occupier power only over security matters, the government has refined its control by means of more than 1,000 military orders. Benvenisti's 1982 report concludes that:

> the sum of legislative enactments, judicial changes and administrative arrangements has created a system of government that not only negates the Geneva Convention but also the principles laid out by the Israeli High Court. . . .[5]

The most severe restrictions have been placed upon freedom of expression, movement, assembly, and, of course, independent rule. To inhibit the development of a West Bank economy, equally severe restrictions are placed on land reclamation, development of water resources, importation of machinery, credit facilities and capital investment.

The last elections on the West Bank were in 1976—under Israeli sponsorship. In eight of the eleven largest cities, the mayors then elected have since been removed,* replaced in five cases by Israeli citizens. Two were deported. Others are confined to their communities or at other locations.**

"All political activity is forbidden in the occupied territories," states the *Human Rights Report*, "the 'Village Leagues' being the only exception".[6] Village League members, the only West Bank Palestinians permitted to carry arms, are generally viewed as "quislings" by West Bankers. Israeli-conducted polls indicate they enjoy the support of less than one percent of West Bankers.

Censorship is essentially for political rather than security reasons.[7] In May 1982 a news story was censored which reported the seizure by authorities from the Gaza Palestinian Women's Club of sixty-four books as well as a map of Palestine which had been in the Club's offices since 1964.[8]

In 1982 prohibited books numbered over 1,000, including George Orwell's *1984*. Currently banned books include *Israeli Theory of Security and the Previous War* by Zeev Schiff, noted Israeli correspondent for *Ha'aretz*,† and *The Establishment and Formation of the IDF* (Israeli Defense Forces) by Yigal Allon, the famous Israeli General and former Israeli Foreign Minister.[9]

---

* Bireh, Doura, Halhoul, Hebron, Jenin, Nablus, Qalqilya, Ramallah. Two remain in office (Bethlehem, Tulkarm).

**In November 1983 Bassam Sha'ka, deposed Mayor of Nablus, was denied permission to travel to Jerusalem to accept an invitation to meet with a visiting British dignitary. In 1982 Elias Freij, Mayor of Bethlehem, was denied permission to travel to the United States to appear on NBC's "Meet The Press".

†There are references herein to various Israeli periodicals, including the newspapers *Al-Hamishmar, Davar, Ha'aretz, The Jerusalem Post, Yediot Aharonot* and the weekly magazines *Ha'ir* and *Koterit Rashit*.

'ORWELLIAN' EDICT BY AREAS COMMANDER

To the Editor of The Jerusalem Post

Sir, —"By virtue of my powers as IDF commander in the (Judea and Samaria) region, believing it to be for the welfare of the population (sic!) and in order to protect the sources of water and the agricultural produce of the region for the benefit of the public, I hereby order as follows . . . No person shall plant a fruit tree unless he has previously obtained a permit in writing from the competent authority . . ."

This is not, as might be expected, a rather inept lampoon on what is going on in the West Bank. It is real. The facsimile of order 1015 of the commander of IDF in the territories was reproduced in a recent number of the weekly *Koteret Rashit*. The order goes on to provide that the existence of every tree which had been planted when the order was promulgated be reported to the authorities within 90 days. "Unreported" trees may be uprooted; offenders are liable to one year's imprisonment.

This is not just another bureaucratic measure to harass the inhabitants or a means by which to reward "good" Arabs and penalize "bad" ones. To obtain a permit, the applicant will have to prove ownership of the land concerned, a burden which, in the faulty state of land registration in the territories, it will often be impossible to lift. Blooming orchards may thus eventually turn barren and then, under Jordanian law, become public domain.

Order 1039 has amended order 1015 so that "fruit trees" now include also vegetables.

Needless to say, these orders do not, "of course," apply to Jews; they do not have to conserve water.

It may not be inappropriate to remind readers of this Machiavellian (and Orwellian) edict, of the Camp David Accord reached just six years ago. Mr. Begin and Mr. Sadat agreed ". . . there shall be transitional arrangements for the West Bank and Gaza for a period not exceeding five years. In order to provide full autonomy to the inhabitants under these arrangements, the Israeli military government and its civilian administration will be withdrawn as soon as a self-governing authority has been freely elected by the inhabitants of these areas to replace the existing military government. . . ."

MICHAEL J. BERGER

Jerusalem.

The observations of Mr. Berger, in the above letter to the Editor, THE JERUSALEM POST *(International Edition), October 2-8, 1983, with respect to Orders 1015 and 1039 are substantially correct. The Orders presently apply only to plum trees, grapes, tomato and eggplants. All commercial planting (and planting for personal consumption in excess of twenty) of the specified trees and plants is prohibited except with a permit. The official explanation that the orders are to "protect the sources of water" is difficult to understand, since irrigation is not used by West Bank farmers for plums and grapes. These fruits are rain fed. As for tomatoes and eggplants, these plants were already denied new water by the authorities. With but a few exceptions, during the sixteen years of military occupation West Bankers have not been permitted to drill wells for irrigation.*

People are punished in the occupied territories, observes the *Human Rights Report*, "without there being any obligation to explain the reason to them," and Israel imposes a "black-out" on events in these areas. Respecting collective punishment the report concludes:

> Continued rule has allowed Israel to 'perfect' methods of punishment. . . . The outstanding characteristic is the extensive, almost daily use of collective punishment. . . . It is difficult to find evidence that these measures changed Israel's ability to preserve order. [10]

The most common forms of collective punishment are curfews, the closing of stores or their forced openings, the demolition or sealing shut of homes, and travel restrictions on group meetings. In 1980 seventeen homes were demolished and eleven sealed; in 1981 seventeen were demolished and seven sealed; in 1982 thirty five were demolished or sealed. [11]

In many cases, destruction of the home precedes the court trial of the suspect. House demolition is generally carried out shortly after the order is given to the family, often within an hour or two. There is no monetary compensation for a person whose home is destroyed. [12]

"The demolition of three houses in Hebron," the editor of *Davar* commented, "marks a return to the forgotten method of collective punishment," and, furthermore, that:

> The fact that all the young people who were arrested are mere suspects, did not stop the security forces from demolishing and sealing their houses and by so doing, harming their parents and siblings who are now left homeless. Waiting for the verdict, as was the rule in the past, seemed, this time, too long somehow.

Israeli law is extended to settlers in the occupied territories, while Palestinians remain under military rule.* "In almost every encounter between members of the two communities," concludes the *Human Rights Report*, "preference for the Jew is *a priori* guaranteed by law."

> The State of Israel granted settlers in the West Bank a complex, unknown status. In addition to their status as citizens taking Israeli law with them across sovereign Israeli borders, they also comprise part of the executive powers, responsible for preserving public law and order. With the State's assistance and backing, these residents view themselves as fulfilling the function of a 24-hour-a-day police. [13]

Avraham Ahituv, the former head of General Security Services (Shin Bet, the branch of Israel's intelligence service responsible for internal security), has described the West Bank settlements as a "psychological

---

*Though a civilian administration was established in November 1981, it is still subject to the authority of the military government and the controls over the Palestinian population were in no way diminished.

THE USE AND ABUSE OF LAW

Zahira Kamal can't sleep late even one morning a week. Every day, seven days in a week, she must present herself at the police station at 7:30 in the morning, and seven hours later, at 2:30, she must appear again at the police station. She then has another three hours of 'freedom' to move around before the sun sets and she must stay at home until the next morning. For the last three years, Zahira Kamal, a lecturer in a local college, has been under house arrest.

Up until four years ago, Zahira 38, single, a graduate of Cairo University (physics and research methods) lived in relative peace with the Israeli occupation authorities. In August 1979, she was ordered to appear for the first time in her life, for questioning by Israeli security. The questioning produced nothing and she was released four hours later.

A few days later, in the middle of the night, they came to her house with a search order. They confiscated books, newspapers and written materials which were never returned. The next day she was taken to the police station and told she was under administrative arrest. Four and a half months later she was released.

She was never brought before a judge. No charges were made against her. She was never told why she was arrested, or freed.

For the next half year she enjoyed the unlimited freedom (at least apparently) enjoyed by every Israeli citizen in a democratic state. At the beginning of 1980, they returned. Again at night. Again with an order—this time of restriction. The order read:

> In accordance with the authority granted me by regulation 6 (2) and 110 of the Emergency Regulations, deeming it necessasry for the public security and defence of the state, I, Col. Amnon Shahak, order Zahira Kamal of Wadi Joz, East Jerusalem placed under police surveillance for six months. She must live in Jerusalem. She may not leave the area without the written permission of the district police commandant. She must present herself twice a day at the nearest police headquarters at any hour demanded. She must remain in her house from sundown to sunup, and the police may visit at any time.
>
> Col. Amnon Shahak,
> Head of the Central Command

Since then the order has been renewed automatically six times—three years. . . .

From 1980 until 1982, 219 restriction orders were issued against 107 people, some of them Israelis. Today, about 70 people are under restriction orders. . . .

Yediot Aharonot, December 23, 1983

hothouse for the growth of Jewish terror."[14]

Following the fatal stabbing of a Jewish student in Hebron in mid-1983, the editor of *The Jerusalem Post* was prompted to write:

> The grim events . . . prove that the situation . . . has totally gone out of control. . . .
>
> [A] number of questions have to be asked. . . . Why did the army

YOU CAN ONLY WEEP

A few days after a gang of Jewish thugs uprooted several dozen electricity poles in Hebron, I met a prominent Palestinian from the town. An academic, speaking excellent English, he related quietly, calmly and in measured and precise words how he had been stripped naked and ordered to stand motionless on the same spot for fifty-six hours in the course of a certain investigation. Prior to that, he said, he had been tied to the rail of an open window and had a hose pipe trained on him. A few days later he was released, after being told that he had been detained in error.

Asked what he did on his release, he replied that he went home. When asked what we Israelis who oppose such methods of investigation could do, after a moment's hesitation he said, in his soft voice and moderate tone: "You can weep: weep for what the occupation authorities are doing to us and weep for what they are making of your society. You can weep—as the soldier who brought me food in my cell wept. You can weep as Israel Galili wept, at the meeting with your Prime Minister when he learned of the violence done to the civilian population of the conquered territories. Beyond that you can do nothing."

When we protested that Israel is still a democratic country where publicity and journalistic coverage of such deeds have an effect, he laughed and said: "You are wrong. You are living in a dream world. Here on the West Bank, even the will and intentions of Mr. Begin are without value or effect. Here on the West Bank it is not the Israeli government that rules, nor Israeli law. Here there is another regime altogether, run by faceless, anonymous people from your security services, by military governors and gangs of settlers who behave as if they owned everything, without fear of any law. The regime whose whims we are subject to," he concluded, "does not give a damn for the government of Israel, the Knesset or Israeli law. Really, you can only weep. . . ."

Yehoshua Sobol, Israeli writer and journalist
Al-Hamishmar, May 16, 1983

reinforcements stand idly by when Jewish settlers attacked and burned down most of the stalls of the Hebron market, despite the fact that a curfew was imposed on the town immediately after the murder ? . . .

[T]he Jewish settlers under the leadership of nationalist fanatics such as Rabbi Levinger have again forced the government's hand into acting against Hebron's appointed mayor without applying the law against their own lawlessness. . . .[15]

The *Human Rights Report* classifies three types of settler violence against the local populace: (1) action not requiring prior organization; (2) preplanned punitive measures such as breaking car windows and puncturing tires; and (3) "acts demanding greater sophistication, technical knowledge, confidentiality from the surroundings, conspirative organizing and intelligence information."[16]

The attitudes of extremist settlers have received publicity. "I give them [the Palestinians] the option," said Rabbi Meir Kahane, "leave with money within the year or leave later, dead and without money."[17] What is not generally appreciated is that the attitude of many Israeli leaders is sometimes not dissimilar. Former Prime Minister Begin referred to Palestinians as "two-legged animals". General Rafael Eitan, for six years Chief of Staff, is reported to have remarked that, after more Israeli settlements, "all the Arabs will be able to do will be to scurry around like drugged cockroaches in a bottle."[18] The Deputy Speaker of the Knesset said that Israel made a "calamitous mistake" in 1967 when it did not drive 200,000 to 300,000 Palestinians out of the West Bank, as, he said, Palestinians had been driven from Lod, Ramle, and the Galilee in 1948.[19]

"Perhaps the worst sign" that "an ill wind is blowing against the direction of the Zionist vision," says Amnon Rubinstein, former Dean of the Tel Aviv University Law School, "is that it is becoming hard to distinguish between the lunatic fringe and the mainstream of our political life...."[20]

The *Human Rights Report* published a memorandum of a meeting at the office of the Civil Administration for the West Bank, setting forth policy toward "Radicals" (presumably those favoring an independent Palestinian state) and pro-Jordanians (presumably those favoring a West Bank relationship with Jordan). The memorandum read:

POLICY VIS-A-VIS "RADICALS" AND "JORDANISTS"

GROUP 1 *("Mayors and Radicals")* Continuation of the battle with the nationalists. This is a continual battle to be incessantly pursued with great devotion against the entire group. This is the task first and foremost of the military governors and all of the military (pressure on this group is not to be stopped after they are removed from their positions) . . . Each of the staff officers should offer suggestions on dealing with them.

GROUP 2 *("Jordanists or pro-Jordanians. These include a number of mayors and heads of chambers of commerce and others who are pragmatic moderates in their political leadership")* Continued maximum neutralization, making them greatly dependent on the civil administration. Shall be dealt with by imposing sanctions and by removal en masse of those detrimental to the system. . . . The staff officers shall recommend who will be dismissed by forced retirement or through disciplinary court.[21]

The Report then cited court testimony of the Chief of Staff that he ordered collective punishment and harassment ("arrest and release, arrest and release"), as well as officer testimony of instructions to "shoot at water tanks on the rooftops and to break watches," to assemble residents indiscriminately, put them in buses and drive until the gasoline runs out, to gather men, ages 18-26, and have soldiers "beat them on their arms and legs" with clubs.[22]

Palestinians are deeply concerned that the actions of settler-vigilantes, using arms supplied by the military, coupled with a breakdown in military discipline, will expose them to sophisticated techniques of violence.

Writes West Bank lawyer Jonathan Kuttab:

> The mood among [West Bank] Palestinians is highly volatile—frightened, confused, fatalist, resentful, at times even hysterical. The extremist plan to expel us from the territories may seem incredible, but to us it looks more plausible every day. The longer Israel retains the territories and denies our national aspirations, the quicker such horrible plans will become not only possible but inevitable.[23]

Many Israelis share Mr. Kuttab's views. Said journalist Dani Rubinstein in early 1982:

> I think one can find more expression of dislike of Arabs than used to be the case in the past, and there is the cumulative effect of many years of hostility and wars with the Arabs. We see racism and militancy among the younger generation at the universities, for example. A high school student told me at a lecture: "Why are we so righteous and apologetic? In 1948 we drove the Arabs away." It is not only the younger generation that reminds us of the 1948 events. Those events are referred to at political debates. Several years ago Moshe Dayan said that the Jewish moshav Nahalal was built where the Arab village Ma'alul once stood. And after [former Prime Minister] Yitzhak Rabin published his book *Service Diary*, one talked about the expulsion of Arabs from Lod and Ramle. These and other instances of recalling the past are more than a hint concerning the present: if they did so in the past, why not today as well? . . .
>
> The reason for these ideas is the now prevalent position in Israel that Eretz Israel shall never be divided again. Then it is obvious that one must have a "solution" for the Arabs who live here without accepting our rule. These ideas, even when they do not reflect any practical plans to expel the Arabs, are the price we pay for the settlements in the West Bank and its de facto annexation to Israel. It is not only a depressing moral price, difficult for many of us to take; it is also a practical price of losing the support of public opinion and governments in Western Europe and the United States on which we are so dependent.[24]

Even those who do not discuss the risk of expulsion acknowledge the drift toward an apartheid-like system. Says Peace Now:

> The continuous and systematic violation of international law and international conventions, to which Israel is a signatory, threatens to isolate Israel internationally, severely harming Israel's image and public standing as a law-abiding democratic state. . . .
>
> The evolution of a dual legal system, which distinguishes between two groups of inhabitants residing in the same territory, effectively creates an

apartheid-like system.[25]

The most telling summation of conditions of the occupation is from the pen of the noted Israeli writer, Amos Elon. Elon is the author of the authoritative study, *The Israelis: Founders And Sons.* "What Elon writes," the editors of *Dissent* observed, "is all the more notable, and alarming, because in the Israeli political spectrum he is far from being on the extreme left."[26] Wrote Elon:

> Today we are a 'democracy of masters,' and we are progressing toward apartheid — because of what is happening . . . in the West Bank's cities and villages.
>
> The fact is that today we have a dual system of law, justice and administration: a free one for the Israelis and a totalitarian one for the Arab inhabitants of Judea and Samaria and the Gaza Strip. The former enjoy freedom of speech, publication and press; the latter do not. And if they open their mouths, the authorities may throw them in jail for an unlimited period, or exile them. The former are punished for their misdeeds; the latter, for opinions. The former can move freely, buy property and land, settle anywhere in the breadth of the land of Israel; the latter cannot, but are limited to the 'Pale,' like the Jews of Czarist Russia or the blacks of South Africa. . . .
>
> The first group lives in a parliamentary democracy; the other under total military rule. . . . The one lives in a country governed by more or less systematic law; the other in a police state of arbitrary orders that usually cannot be appealed. The one is more or less protected from raging hooligans; the other is exposed to the violence of private militias [the Israeli settlers in the Occupied Territories] that take the law into their own hands, carrying out illegal arrests, destroying houses, seizing property and desecrating holy places. The one is considered to be living in its own country; the other is advised to emigrate for *its* good and for *ours*. Who remembers when this recently happened to the Jews?
>
> The most crucial story of our lives today is here, and in the continuing refusal of many among us to see things as they are, repressing them from our consciousness. Many Israelis — perhaps a majority — have renounced their political and moral responsibilities, as decent Germans did when the Nazis came to power.[27]

FOOTNOTES

1   Flapan, *Zionism And The Palestinians, supra,* p. 12.
2   *Ibid.,* p. 11.
3   "This Week with David Brinkley," ABC News, April 10, 1983.
4   *Human Rights, supra,* p. 2.
5   Benvenisti, *The West Bank and Gaza Data Base Project, supra,* p. 40.
6   *Human Rights, supra,* p. 144.
7   *Ibid.,* p. 171.
8   Nat Hentoff, "The Censors Of The West Bank," *Inquiry,* February 1984.
9   *Human Rights, supra,* p. 139.
10 *Ibid.,* p. 167, 168.
11 *Ibid.,* p. 157.
12 *Ibid.,* p. 157.
13 *Ibid.,* p. 166.
14 *The Jerusalem Post* (International Edition), August 28-September 3, 1983.
15 *The Jerusalem Post,* July 10, 1983.
16 *Human Rights, supra,* pp. 57, 58.
17 *Ha'ir,* February 25, 1983; Asa Kasher, *Koteret Rashit,* April 4, 1983. Dr. Kasher is Professor of Philosophy, Tel Aviv University.
18 David Shipler, "The Israeli Army Signs A Political Truce," *The New York Times,* May 15, 1983.
19 *The Jerusalem Post* (International Edition), March 20-26, 1983. Also reported in *Ha'aretz,* March 17, 1983, and *Al Hamishmar,* March 20, 1983.
20 *Ha'aretz,* March 19, 1982.
21 *Human Rights, supra,* p. 64.
22 *Ibid.,* p. 65.
23 Jonathan Kuttab, "West Bank Arabs Foresee Expulsion," *The New York Times,* August 1, 1983.
24 Dani Rubinstein, "Preparing For Expulsion," *Davar,* February 26, 1982.
25 *Everything You Didn't Want To Know, supra.*
26 "Shame On The West Bank," *Dissent,* Spring 1983.
27 Nat Hentoff, "The Continuing Silence Of Most American Jews," *The Village Voice,* June 7, 1983.

V. *Israeli Opposition to the West Bank Settlements*

ON THE ISSUE OF SETTLEMENT EXPANSION in the West Bank, Prime Minister Begin stood firm against "the mainstream of Israeli scholars, intellectuals and writers,"[1] as well as the aims of Presidents Jimmy Carter and Ronald Reagan.

Begin's Israeli critics argued that annexation would dilute Israel's Jewish character and compromise its democratic principles. Confusing ideology with security, furthermore, would jeopardize Israel's security. "Settlements serve no useful purpose except to threaten the Arabs all around with disinheritance," *The Jerusalem Post* editorialized.[2] Even if the 100,000 settlement goal for the West Bank is achieved, said Hirsch Goodman, "the ratio of Arab to Jew on the West Bank will be eight-to-one in the Arabs favor."[3] (The current Arab-Jewish ratio in the Gaza Strip is close to 500-to-1.)

Following a U.S. veto in August 1983 of a UN resolution criticizing the settlements, *The Jerusalem Post* observed:

> Mr. Reagan, facing another presidential contest, may find it useful to throw hints that he would be looking the other way if Israel goes on erecting settlements. But Israelis do not have that option. . . .[4]

One of the most distinguished of Prime Minister Begin's critics was the Israeli historian J. L. Talmon, described by Rabbi Arthur Hertzberg as one of the "greatest Jewish political thinkers of our time". Shortly before his death in 1980, Talmon wrote:

> There is nothing more contemptible and harmful than the use of religious sanctions in a conflict between nations. . . .
>
> A religious claim is valid when it relates to matters between people and their creator—to prayer, fast, atonement, faith, and ritual. It does, however, inspire opposition if it disregards others' claims and assumes the right to impose its way, or to harm the rights, freedoms, and interests of others. A religious claim will give a strong impression of hubris, an ambition of mastery, if it tries to subordinate the believers of one religion to those of another. It is one thing for the believer to remain within the boundaries of debate over passages in his holy books and theological commentaries; it is quite another if behind him stand tanks, planes, missiles, soldiers, and police, ready to use direct or indirect violence.

Whoever speaks of the need for one people to rule over another for security reasons leads his audience astray. To do so is to sit deliberately on a volcano; it is a source of insecurity and perpetual alarm. The rebellious hostility of a subjected population, particularly if it is supported by millions on the other side of the border, neutralizes any degree of security provided by holding on to this hill or that stream, a strait or marsh, in an age of long-range missiles and bombs. There is something repulsive in the kind of cynicism or naivete that claims that settlements are needed to create conditions of coexistence, while everyone knows that for the Arabs each settlement is another sign of dispossession and gradual conquest. The Jewish image suffers as a result of such double-talk that does nothing to enhance our security or honor.[5]

ISRAEL AT THE BEGINNING OF THE YEAR 5744

Fifteen years ago, some two years after the Six Day War (1967), when a great majority of Israelis, and even a large part of Diaspora Jewry were surfeiting themselves with a barbarous nationalism, arrogance and conceit over military achievements, and visions of "the greatness and the glory and the might forever" of messianic salvation, I dared to explicitly express—in speech and in writing— the suspicion that this wondrous victory that brought in its wake the conquest (or the "liberation") of all the land of Greater Israel and the Sinai Peninsula, will be viewed in the eyes of future historians as the starting point of the decline and fall of the State of Israel. It was clear to me that it was not the territories that was the problem but the people who were living on it—the people we are trying to subjugate and that the inclusion of a population of one and a half million Arabs under Israeli rule, in addition to the half million Arab citizens, would cancel the nature of the state as a Jewish state; that this reality would distance the state both from the history of the Jewish people and from the Jewish people living today throughout society; that it would destroy the personality of the Jew who would become a colonial conqueror; and that it would destroy any chance for reconciliation (or co-existence) with the world in whose midst we are destined to exist, and that it would drag us into additional wars until the bitter end—the ultimate war with the entire Arab world (and don't console yourselves today about the inner divisions within the Arab world, they are no worse than our own inner divisions). In this same war, that will surely come in the aftermath of our rule over the Palestinian nation, the sympathy of the whole world will be on the Arab side.

At that time, there was almost no understanding of this apprehension within any part of the public. But today, in this context, I am flooded by letters and visits from Jews of all political camps, the majority of them youth, who come to express their anguish, at times reaching despair, over what they recognized as our political and social reality today and over what they feel about this reality; and they choose to engage me in dialogue because I was one of the first to express what they recognize and sense only now.

Mattityahu Peled, speaking from his experience as an IDF Major General, argued that expanded borders were not required for Israel's security:

> To begin with, it's a big mistake to believe that the borders we had until 1967 were imposed borders. They were not. These were the borders we Israelis really elected. We chose them. . . . After 1967, the appetite grew with the eating, and the whole argument that Israel cannot look for guaranteed security without additional territory is a sheer lie.[6]

Meron Benvenisti urged the wisdom of partition:

> For partition to work, the map must be drawn along demographic lines—

. . . From the point of view of what [a citizen of Israel] sees and feels every day, Jewish statehood is reflected only in the military activity of conquest, which is not aimed at defending the state of the Jewish people, but at preserving the "whole Eretz Israel," which will never be the state of the Jewish people since another people also lives there. While neglecting positive tasks and the duty of dealing with its internal problems, the state sacrifices its might, its capital and the blood of its sons on the altar of building settlements in the occupied territories, by developing a caste of professional armed settlers whose task is to intimidate the subjugated Arab population.

In the name of the establishment of rule over another nation and in the name of the suppression of their natural desire for liberation from subordination to Israel, it becomes necessary to use ever more cruel means of oppression, approaching barbarism (in the words of a member of the Supreme Court of Israel). But also within the Jewish nation as well, which lives in a political-social framework where this violence is part of the government and army, the view of violence as a norm in human relationships is spreading. . . .

Against this background of accommodation to oppression, violence and exploitation of the other, one sees increasing hooliganism in Jewish society, both in relations between men and between the individual and his society—and over it all hovers nationalism and patriotism. As a poet and philosopher of the nineteenth century once said, the path leading from humanity to bestiality passes through nationalism.

. . . As to the fate of the state, this depends on whether or not a solution will be found to the problem of the existence of two peoples in this country, each of which is deeply conscious of the fact that the country is his. For this tragic reality, there is only one of two solutions: either the catastrophic solution of war until the bitter end, or the division of the country between the two peoples. There is no third way.

YESHAYAHU LEIBOWITZ, Orthodox scholar and Israeli Professor of Philosophy
Ha'aretz, September 16, 1983*

*Israeli Press Briefs, No. 17, October, 1983, International Center for Peace in the Middle East, Tel Aviv, and "From The Israeli Press," *Journal Of Palestine Studies*, Winter, 1984, p. 169.

Jews here, Arabs there. The more two populations become intermingled, the harder it will be. So if you continue putting major Jewish settlements in Arab areas, you finish the possibility of partition. It becomes impossible—unless, of course, you're willing to create yet another refugee problem.[7]

In 1978 the best known of the various organizations in the Israeli peace movement, Peace Now, was organized by a group of reserve officers, some of whom had been decorated for gallantry in the 1973 War. It has garnered considerable national support and attracted international attention. Through its aggressive challenge to the moral, ideological and economic basis for the government's settlement policy, it is responsible for some of the largest protests against that policy in Israeli history. It has pointed out the crippling cost of the settlements and how they weigh upon the country's social system. It has cast severe doubt on the ability of the country to support the continued West Bank occupation. Says Peace Now:

> The annexation of the West Bank is a terrifying prospect, which is gradually unfolding before our very eyes. In another five—or even three—years, 100,000 Jewish settlers will reside on the West Bank. . . .
> - What political agreement can be reached after Israel effectively annexes the West Bank?
> - What will be the fate of the 1.3 million Arab inhabitants of the territories?
> - What will be the face of Israel as an annexationist society?
> - On what are we expending 3 billion dollars? Are there not other, more worthy goals for such monumental investments?
>
> IT SEEMS CLEAR THAT THE TASK OF HALTING SETTLEMENT AND ANNEXATION HAS BECOME A MATTER OF SHEER SURVIVAL.[8]

The frustration of many Israelis and their hope for outside assistance is reflected in the remarks of Dr. Meir Pa'il, a military historian who was both a Knesset member and Director of the Military Academy (Israel's West Point). Said Dr. Pa'il:

> As a result of the Israeli policies of the last generation, there can be no doubt that a cancerous disease . . . has attacked the very heart of the Zionist enterprise. Only peace and a solution to the Palestinian problem can uproot this cancer. Israel must offer the Arab world the territories she conquered in June 1967 in exchange for peace and demilitarization arrangements. She must then take her place within the family of Middle Eastern nations and work to transform this peace treaty into a friendship treaty. . . .
>
> [If] Israeli public opinion remains glued to its present course, then the best remaining option would be for the superpowers (or at least one of them) to force Israel to evacuate the territories for peace. In the present state of the Zionist enterprise, *a coerced peace is better than a freely chosen war.* For if peace does not come to Israel before the end of the 20th century, the Zionist enterprise may not live out the 21st.[9]

After a visit to Israel in 1982, *New York Times* Editorial Page Editor, Max Frankel, reported that the opposition to Begin was "reduced to begging America to break Mr. Begin's political power. And it now advocates means that would have been unthinkable even a few weeks ago. The startling plea of many leading Israelis [is] that the United States *reduce* its economic aid to their nation. . . ."[10] "[L]eading opposition figures now risk political oblivion," continued Mr. Frankel, "by counseling sharp cuts in America's nonmilitary aid of $800 million a year. . . . Mr. Begin will go on bribing the electorate, his critics say, until his West Bank ambition—underwritten by the American tax-payer—is finally achieved."[11]

In August 1983 one hundred leading Israeli public figures, including thirty members of the Knesset and a majority of the Labor Alignment, united in opposing the government's settlement policy which they warned:

▶ endangers the security of Israel, contributes to a perpetuation of the conflict and a vicious circle of violence, of suffering, repression and bloodshed;

▶ will frustrate any prospect of arriving at a peaceful solution to the conflict so long as Israel continues to rule over a foreign population and prevents them from realizing their national aspirations;

▶ runs counter to Israel's character as a democratic Jewish state;

▶ diverts resources from vital sectors such as economic development and aid to the underprivileged in development towns, city slums and other depressed areas;

▶ corrupts the soul of the people of Israel, deepens the cleavage within the country and encourages anti-democratic, extremist tendencies;

▶ isolates Israel from the democratic community and alienates the Jews of the Diaspora. *

Their statement concluded:

We call upon the government of Israel to put an end to this ruinous policy, to halt the building of new settlements, to remove this obstacle to the peace process and to encourage negotiations towards a solution which will ensure the security of Israel without negating the rights of other people.

Whatever the reasons—repercussions from the Lebanese invasion, deteriorating economic conditions and a 300 percent rate of inflation, or the criticism from Israeli intellectual and political leaders, the U.S. government and the world Jewish community—public opinion in Israel is changing on the settlement issue. This is shown most dramatically by polls of *Ha'aretz* (often called *The New York Times* of Israel).

*See Appendix D.

On the question of further settlements in the West Bank, the response has been:

	Opposed to further settlement	In support of further settlement
October, 1981	29.2%	58.3%
October 8, 1982	34.5%	48.5%
December 28, 1983	48.5%	36.9%

FOOTNOTES

1   Howe, "The West Bank Trap," *supra.*
2   *The Jerusalem Post,* January 14, 1980.
3   Goodman, "Home Is Where The West Bank Is," *supra.*
4   *The Jerusalem Post* (International Edition), August 7-13, 1983.
5   J. L. Talmon, "The Homeland Is In Danger," *Dissent,* Fall 1980. See Appendix H.
6   "Israel On The Edge Of Elections," *The Village Voice,* May 27, 1981.
7   Quoted in Fein, "What, Then, Shall We Do?," *supra.*
8   Ofira Seliktar, "The Cost Of Vigilance In Israel: Linking The Economic And Social Costs Of Defense," *Journal Of Peace Research,* No. 4, Vol. XVII, 1980.
9   *Everything You Didn't Want To Know, supra.*
10 Meir Pa'il, "Zionism Today. Zionism In Danger Of Cancer (Part Two)," *New Outlook,* January, 1984.
11 Max Frankel, The Editorial Notebook, "Looming Over The West Bank," *The New York Times,* November 15, 1982.
12 Max Frankel, The Editorial Notebook, "Help Us By Cutting Aid," *The New York Times,* November 16, 1982.

VI. *American Jewish Opposition to the Settlements*

AS ISRAELI SETTLEMENT ACTIVITY on the West Bank grew in the years following the 1967 war, so did concern in the American Jewish community that Israel's policies would make ultimate peace between Israel and the Palestinians more difficult.

One organization early to recognize that the conflict was between Palestinian nationalism and Jewish nationalism was Breira ("Alternative"), founded in 1973. Rabbi David Saperstein, a Breira Executive Committee member, is quoted as saying: "We must make people understand that they can continue to be strong supporters of Israel even if they feel morally they must speak out for the national rights of the Palestinians."[1] Breira, noted the *American Jewish Yearbook:*

> had been vocal in its criticism of the Israeli government for its handling of the Israel-Palestinian conflict. Although *Breira* never achieved a membership of more than 1,500, its ability to attract some individuals prominent in the rabbinate, on campuses and in the Jewish institutional world, and the public relations skills of some of its spokesman, had enabled *Breira* to get considerable press coverage for its views. *Breira* encountered intensive criticism in early 1977 from several Anglo-Jewish publications, which attacked not only the substance of its positions, but impugned the motives of its advocates.[2]

Many Jewish organizations and institutions ostracized Breira personnel and some extreme Jewish groups resorted to violence to disrupt Breira meetings. By 1978 pressure from the organized Jewish community had rendered Breira ineffective.[3]

The same *Yearbook* described attitudes among American Jews following Prime Minister Begin's election in 1977:

> Begin's election, his more active settlement policy, and his outspoken opposition to territorial compromise on the West Bank aroused misgivings among many American Jews. Rabbi Schindler and the leaders of such intergroup relations organizations as the American Jewish Committee, the American Jewish Congress, and the Anti-Defamation League of B'nai B'rith spoke privately with Begin and other members of his government to convey their concern over the difficulties they were encountering in explaining certain Israeli policies and tactics to the American public. However, these

misgivings were rarely given public expression during the period under review.[4]

In 1978 Arthur H. Samuelson, former editor of the Breira magazine *InterChange,* described the dilemma of American Jewry. "We are going to have a hard time selling this [settlement] policy because we do not believe it will work," he quotes one organization staff member as explaining, "but it is Israel's policy and we have the duty to support it no matter what."[5] Samuelson then noted the reaction of Rabbi Balfour Brickner of the Stephen Wise Free Synagogue, New York, to the "advertising agency approach" of selling Israeli policy:

> There is a basic schizophrenia in American Jewry. We hide behind the argument that it is not for us to speak our minds, because the Israelis have to pay the price, but I think that is precisely why we have to speak out when we spot trouble—to save Jewish lives.
>
> Why is it that Israeli school-children can write an open letter to Begin, saying his policy raises doubts in their minds as to Israel's sincerity for peace; and why is it that 300 veteran officers can publish an advertisement in the Israeli press, saying that if Begin persists on the settlements issue they will have to draw conclusions as to the justness of Israel's cause; . . . What we need is for several big givers to the UJA to threaten to stop contributing if Israel does not retreat from its suicidal position. That is the only language the Israelis understand.[6]

Samuelson further quoted from a *Ha'aretz* interview with Lawrence Tisch, in which that major contributor to the United Jewish Appeal is reported saying:

> There was never such an idiotic approach taken by an Israeli Government toward the settlements in the occupied territories. The Jews will always support Israel, even when they do not agree with her, but the American public is a different story. . . .
>
> The only thing that Israel has to offer is the justness of her cause. American Jews can influence American public opinion only when they can prove they are fighting for a just cause. We can fight for border adjustments or a fair settlement, but when Israel is wrong, we lose our power. If Begin insists on pressing the settlement issue, he will lose every last American. There is no justification for his position. . . .[7]

Continued Samuelson: "A few U.S. Jews are tiring of private representations and communications and are beginning to speak out. They are usually intellectuals who do not depend on the Jewish community for either their livelihood or their reputation." He cited Irving Howe as saying:

> I think that the Israeli position on the settlements is absolutely indefensible. Except for those people who have received word from heaven that Judea and Samaria belong to the Jews—and with such people it is impossible to argue—supporters of Israel have to recognize that if there is to be peace in

the Middle East, sooner or later—and with all kinds of cautions and qualifications—Israeli domination of the West Bank has to end. This means that the Israeli Government has to give up the idea that it has a right to the domination of the West Bank, let alone to sovereignty over the West Bank.[8]

A Jewish leader's view of the role of the Conference of Presidents of Major Jewish Organizations was noted by Samuelson:

We American Jews have no real political strategy of our own when it comes to Israeli-American relations. The Presidents' Conference does not deal with substantive political issues, only with public relations difficulties which arise in defending Israeli policy. The conference has never gone to President Carter and said, we believe this and this as Americans and this is the policy we would like you to pursue. Instead, it acts like a third-rate messenger boy for the Israeli Embassy, only providing the Israeli reaction to events, never proposing alternatives.[9]

The Conference of Presidents declined President Sadat's request in January 1978 to meet with them and one organization after another denounced his "open letter" in the American press calling upon American Jews to support his peace efforts.[10]

In February 1978 a delegation representing the Union of American Hebrew Congregations, the American Jewish Committee, the American Jewish Congress, the Anti-Defamation League and the National Jewish Community Relations Advisory Council met to discuss how best to inform visiting Foreign Minister Moshe Dayan of their assessment of the damage being done to Israel by the planting of new settlements. They were rejected and criticized by Mr. Dayan.[11]

In June 1979 fifty-nine prominent American Jewish figures, known for their ardent support of Israel, petitioned Begin to reconsider his settlement policy. In a letter to the Prime Minister, they wrote:

We are profoundly distressed, however, by the decision of your government to create new settlements on the West Bank.... [A] policy which requires the expropriation of Arab land unrelated to Israel's security needs, and which presumes to occupy permanently a region populated by over 750,000 Palestinian Arabs, we find morally unacceptable, and perilous for the democratic character of the Jewish state.[12]

A 1980 study by Louis Harris and Associates, Inc. for The World Jewish Congress of the attitudes of the American people and the American Jewish community toward the Arab-Israeli conflict determined that 59 percent of American Jews (25 percent opposed) shared the view that "there must be a way to guarantee Israel's security and also give the Palestinians an independent state on the West Bank." (Only 11 percent of the general public disagreed.) The study stated that this was "perhaps the key result in all the questioning about the West Bank."[13]

By 1983 a number of Jewish organizations, despite the anguish accompanying the debate,* had developed constructive positions on the Palestinian issue.

The American Jewish Committee states that it:

> shares the concerns of many Israelis that the continuing and indefinite Israeli administration of the West Bank and Gaza, with governance over the lives of more than a million Arabs who are not citizens of Israel, could in the course of time undermine the democratic and humane principles of the State of Israel.

and also believes that:

> Israel's current settlement policy, if continued, may make withdrawal at a later date no longer a viable option for any Israeli government. . . .**

The Central Conference of American Rabbis certifies that "the legitimate demands of security for Israel can—and must—be reconciled with the dignity, human rights and the right of self-determination of Palestinian Arabs." The Conference has called for "a temporary cessation of further settlement activities on the West Bank.†

New Jewish Agenda, with thirty-five chapters throughout the U.S., calls for mutual recognition by Israel and the Palestinian people, including the right of Palestinian self-determination, and "cessation of further Israeli settlement on the West Bank and Gaza, and an end to the repression of the Palestinians." ††

In 1983 the Committee of Concerned American Jews, organized by Professor Seymour Martin Lipset of Stanford University and former Common Cause President David Cohen among others, solicited 37,000 members of the Jewish community. Voicing the concern of the Committee, Professor Lipset announced:

> If the Committee of Concerned American Jews does nothing else, we intend to make clear that questioning the policies of the government of

---

* In March 1983, a delegation of eighteen rabbis (two Orthodox, several Conservative, the balance Reform) called upon fifteen U.S. Congressional supporters of Israel to advocate a freeze on West Bank settlements. They chose not to hold a press conference or otherwise publicize their effort. Asked afterward whether the meetings were effective, one Rabbi commented, "Even those who didn't share our views appreciated that we came. Some understood our anguish . . . some admitted their difficulty in articulating similar opinions . . . being drowned out by AIPAC [American Israel Public Affairs Committee] or called anti-Semitic or anti-Zionist."[14]

In a June 1983 Jewish Community Hour television discussion of the Lebanese invasion and attitudes in Israel and the American Jewish community, neither the moderator nor any of the four panelists used the word "Palestinian" or mentioned the Palestinian issue.[15]

In the December 1983 issue of the influential magazine *Commentary*, published by the American Jewish Committee, editor Norman Podhoretz, in an article, "The State Of World Jewry," wrote of an "ominous development," *i.e.*, the "resurgence of anti-Zionist ideas and attitudes" in the world Jewish community. Mr. Podhoretz devoted only one sentence in a 9,000 word article to the implications to Israel of its West Bank policies.

**See Appendix F.
† *Ibid.* †† *Ibid.*

Israel does not reflect any dimunition of support for Israel. . . . The fact is that our criticism of Israeli government policies is a reflection of our love and dedication to Israel.

Professor Lipset, however, expressed concern at "the powerful forces within Israel working for policies which place her security in peril" as well as "some efforts in the organized American Jewish community to silence discussion of critical issues affecting Israel and to question the motives of those who dissent."[16]

Professor Lipset previously had written:

> Israel must recognize that it cannot have peace or an end to terrorism without giving the Palestinians the right to self determination. It must recognize that Palestinian nationalism is as legitimate as Jewish nationalism, and hope that there are ways that this nationalism can find expression without threatening Israel.
>
> The only political outcome of the invasion of Lebanon that would give promise of peace would be an offer by Israel to negotiate with the Palestinians on sovereignty in the occupied areas in which they live. The crucial issue is Israeli willingness to grant real self-determination to the West Bank and Gaza.
>
> The views we express here are widespread in Israel, as they are among American Jews. Unfortunately, although Israelis have spoken up in opposition to their Government's policies, American Jews have been largely silent, thereby possibly contributing to the Israeli Government's misperception that American Jews support it in this war.[17]

Another individual to express openly criticism of Israeli policy and to reject the proposition that such discussion would promote anti-Semitism was John B. Oakes, former Senior Editor of *The New York Times*. New York Mayor Koch's criticism of dissenting American Jews prompted Oakes to write:

> The Mayor is a very intelligent man as well as a warm supporter of Israel. As such, he knows that a large body of American Jews who are as sincerely interested in the survivability of the Israeli state as he is are repelled by many policies of the Begin Government—almost as repelled as is the large body of opposition within Israel itself—and we see no reason why we should not say so.
>
> Mayor Koch knows that a great many American Jews as well as a great many other American citizens believe that Prime Minister Begin's apocalpytic intransigence weakens Israel in the long run rather than strengthens it, and thereby increases the danger of renewed war in the Middle East rather than lessens it. This is no more—and no less—than the views held by hundreds of thousands of Israelis themselves. . . .
>
> To imply that American Jews in particular are only promoting anti-Semitism by joining in criticism of this (or any other) Government of Israel is demagogic nonsense. It can only help fuel both the active and the latent anti-Semitism that unfortunately does exist in this and every other country.[18]

Irving Howe, asked, and offered an answer to, a key question:

> What is the ultimate perspective of the Begin people? Don't they realize
> that a takeover of the West Bank can lead only to an endless sequence of
> resistance, sabotage, and armed struggle?
>
> The answer runs, I believe, something like this: They propose to harass
> and humiliate the West Bank Arabs, though they hope not to be too brutal
> about it, so that finally the professionals and intellectuals will leave and
> only the uneducated, easily handled lower classes will remain, traveling each
> day to Jerusalem and Tel Aviv to perform manual labor. This calculation,
> a more humane version of Meyer Kahane's demand that the Arabs simply
> be driven out, is not only morally deplorable, it is politically dubious. For
> the number of educated, troublesome Arabs keeps increasing as West Bank
> society becomes modernized and even peasants now send their sons to the
> universities.[19]

Rabbi Brickner, commenting on the need for new Jewish leadership
in the U.S., pressed Israel to "give up its repressive behavior on the
West Bank". He continued:

> Neither Mr. Begin nor his allies, Professor Milson, Arik Sharon and Rabbi
> Levinger, seem willing, voluntarily, to make that transition. Thus, President
> Reagan will have to apply enormous pressure on Begin in order to alter the
> way the government of Israel interprets the concept of autonomy laid down
> in the Camp David agreement.
>
> Self-determination for the Palestinians remains an undigested lump in
> Israel's belly. The 'victory' in Lebanon won't absorb that lump. The Beirut
> war (as distinct from the Galilee war), initiated to facilitate Israel's annexation
> of the West Bank, may turn out to do just the opposite. . . .[20]

In June 1983 Nat Hentoff reflected upon the American Jewish
community's reluctance to speak out against Israeli policies they believed
antithetical to the development of that state. Citing Amos Elon's stark
summation of West Bank occupation and its dual system of law and
justice, of freedom for Israelis and oppression of Palestinians, Hentoff
asked:

> So where is Elon's passion for justice among most Jews of the United
> States? It is not possible for any Jew who can read to be ignorant of what has
> been going on for so long in the Occupied Territories. Or are these news
> stories biased, anti-Semitic? Then how explain the large, and growing,
> number of critics of these policies among the Jews of Israel? Are they
> self-hating Jews?
>
> Why is it so easy for most American Jews to remain silent? Have the
> invasion of Lebanon, the corpses of children smoking from the phosphorus,
> been thoroughly rationalized by now? Do most American Jews agree with
> the Israeli spokesman who complained last summer on National Public
> Radio that television coverage of that invasion was unfair because all it
> showed was 'people being killed'?
>
> Do most American Jews really not give a damn about whether Israel

becomes the South Africa of the Middle East? Or, put another way, is there *nothing* any Government of Israel can do that would so shock the conscience of most American Jews that they would rise in the synagogues, in the centers, in the Jewish press, in everybody's press — and call that Government of Israel to account?[21]

As 1983 drew to a close, attitudes in the American Jewish community toward the settlements and, equally important , toward the willingness of the Jewish community to discuss the issues openly, had changed substantially from 1978.

A 1983 study of attitudes of American Jews toward Israel and Israelis commissioned by The American Jewish Committee, the "Cohen Report," consisted of two surveys, one of a representative nationwide sample of American Jews, the other of board members of five prominent Jewish communal organizations: the American Jewish Committee, the American Jewish Congress, the Anti-Defamation League, B'nai B'rith, and the United Jewish Appeal.[22]

The study confirmed the depth of the commitment of American Jews to Israel. "Caring about Israel is a very important part of my being a Jew," said 78 percent of the Jewish public and 90 percent of the leaders. "If Israel were destroyed, I would feel as if I had suffered one of the greatest personal tragedies in my life," said 77 percent of the public and 83 percent of the leaders.

The survey opinion most relevant to the settlement issue was the response to the proposal: "Israel should suspend the expansion of settlements in the West Bank to encourage peace negotiations." 51 percent of the American Jewish public (28 percent opposed) and 55 percent of Jewish leaders (25 percent opposed) favored it.*

If American Jewish opinion in 1983 is as strongly opposed to Israel's settlements policy as the polls indicate, what is the explanation for the reluctance of American Jewish leaders to express this view publicly? (Only 42 percent of leaders, compared to 60 percent of the Jewish public, supported the proposition that "American Jewish organizations should feel free to publicly criticize the Israeli government and its policies").

One possible answer was provided by former American Jewish Congress President, Rabbi Arthur Hertzberg. In an interview with the Israeli weekly *Kotoret Rashit*, Hertzberg, after noting that the survey revealed the majority of American Jews to be dovish, was asked why such views were not voiced publicly. He is reported to have replied that "because the Israel government can make or break the political careers of Jewish

---

*The related proposition "Palestinians have a right to a homeland on the West Bank and Gaza, so long as it does not threaten Israel" was supported by 48 percent (26 percent opposed) of the American Jewish public, and by 51 percent (28 percent opposed) of Jewish leaders.

leaders abroad, they prefer to be 'good boys' and follow the official line."[23]

The editor of *Moment*, reflecting upon the Cohen Report, offered a rather thoughtful explanation:

> A good part of the answer may rest with the leaders. Personally, they are substantially more dovish than the public. But they may well view themselves as unable to speak as individuals, given their organizational roles. And they are split down the middle regarding the propriety of criticism when it comes from organizations. So the most visible group of Jews, the group to which the media most often turns for expression of 'the Jewish view,' the group on whom the public most depends for its cues, is also the most inhibited. As Cohen suggests, that inhibition may derive from the seriousness with which the leaders take their organizations. Perhaps they imagine that what an organization says is more likely to be used by Israel's enemies than what an individual says. Or perhaps they fear that an organization that climbs out on a critical limb will lose the support of its constituents. Whatever their reasons, it appears that the leaders—precisely those who regard themselves as best informed about Israel, as most sophisticated in their analysis—feel constrained in expressing their critical conclusions publicly. The leaders, in short, hesitate to lead.[24]

FOOTNOTES

1   Lawrence Mosher, "Israel Worries American Jews," *Middle East International*, June 1976.

2   *American Jewish Yearbook 1979*, The American Jewish Committee, p. 140.

3   Carolyn Toll, "American Jews and the Middle East Dilemma: A struggle waged behind the scenes," *The Progressive*, August, 1979.

4   *The American Jewish Yearbook 1979, supra*, pp. 139-140.

5   Arthur H. Samuelson, "The Dilemma Of American Jewry," *The Nation*, April 1, 1978.

6   *Ibid.* 7 *Ibid.* 8 *Ibid.* 9 *Ibid.* 10 *Ibid.* 11 *Ibid.*

12   See Appendix E. There were many companion public statements from groups of American Jews describing themselves as supporters of Peace Now and espousing, among other things, cessation of further settlements.

13   *A Study of the Attitudes of the American People and the American Jewish Community Toward the Arab-Israeli Conflict in the Middle East*, Louis Harris and Associates, Inc., 1980.

14   Jean Herschaft, *The Jewish Post and Opinion*, March 23, 1983.

15   Jewish Community Hour, Channel 9, Washington, D.C., June 19, 1983.

16   Letter by The Committee of Concerned American Jews, 1983, 910 Independence Avenue, S.E., Washington, D.C. 20003.

17   Nathan Glazer and Seymor Martin Lipset, "Israel Isn't Threatened. The War's Ill-Advised," *The New York Times*, June 30, 1982.

18   John B. Oakes, "Koch's Chutzpah," *The New York Times*, June 21, 1983.

19   Howe, "The West Bank Trap," *supra.*

20   Balfour Brickner, *Sh'ma*, October 1, 1982.

21   Hentoff, "The Continuing Silence of Most American Jews," *supra.*

22   Steven M. Cohen, *Attitudes of American Jews Toward Israel and Israelis, The 1983 National Survey of American Jews and Jewish Communal Leaders*, Institute on American Jewish-Israeli Relations, The American Jewish Committee, 1983.

23   *Newsletter No. 7*, International Center for Peace in the Middle East, Tel Aviv, January 1984.

24   "The Cohen Report: Speaking Hawkish, Feeling Dovish," *Moment*, November 1983.

VII. *The United States and Israel's Settlement Policy*

THE PRESENT ISRAELI GOVERNMENT takes the position that the West Bank and Gaza are not "occupied territories" under UN Security Council Resolution 242. The U.S. and other world powers hold a contrary view.

U.S. administrations prior to that of President Ronald Reagan viewed Israeli settlements in the occupied territories as illegal and as "obstacles to peace".* In 1981 Reagan, while describing them as "unnecessarily provocative," also commented they were "not illegal".** Whether the President intended to signal a substantive change in U.S. policy, his remark was so construed in Israel. Said Dr. Joseph Burg, head of the National Religious Party and Israel's chief negotiator for the autonomy plan called for in the *Camp David Accords:*

> President Reagan did not say the settlements are illegal. That is a difference between this administration and the former administration. That is very important, and if they are not illegal, then surely from our point of view they were legal from the very first day.

Issues involving Israel and Middle East peace are among the most politically sensitive in the United States.† The constraints imposed by this sensitivity often cause U.S. policy to be substantially at variance with world opinion. The late Nahum Goldmann, one of the great Jewish figures of this century who was a president of both the World Jewish Congress and the World Zionist Organization, referred to the "political isolation in which the U.S.A. finds itself, because the Arab

---

* See Appendix A for statement of The Legal Adviser, Department of State, April 21, 1978, that the settlements are "inconsistent with international law." See also, Statement by Ambassador Charles W. Yost, United States Representative to the United Nations, in the Security Council, July 1, 1969 (U.S. Mission to the UN, Press Release USUN-70 (69) July 1, 1969), also included in Moore, *The Arab-Israeli Conflict, supra,* p. 1097.

**See Appendix C for Reagan Administration views on settlements.

† "Historically, American Presidential candidates have avoided criticizing or proposing courses of action that contradict official Israeli policy. Their reluctance has stemmed from a fear of alienating American Jews, who contribute considerable money, time and effort to candidates and who vote in high numbers," Fay S. Joyce, "McGovern Stands Apart, Criticizing Israeli Policy," *The New York Times,* February 4, 1984. The views expressed in March, 1984, by Congressional figures and candidates for office on the bill to move the United States Embassy to Jerusalem reflect this political condition.

countries, the Third World and practically all the European states oppose the American policies with regard to the Middle East."[1] Despite universal disapproval of Israel's settlement program, the U.S. often terms "flawed" the criticism or initiatives of others,* while itself finding difficulty in proposing specific, alternative language or programs to implement its own officially stated opposition.

Despite its opposition to Israeli settlement policy since 1967, the U.S. government can be said to have indirectly subsidized West Bank settlement in which Israel is estimated to have invested $1.5 billion over the last fifteen years.

In a 1983 report to the Congress, the Comptroller General warned that:

> In addition to Israel's rising military debts and other problems, the United States is faced with the possibility of indirectly supporting Israeli actions, with which it does not necessarily agree, through the bolstering of Israeli budget needs. Furthermore, the Israeli Government's liberal subsidies granted to its people for settling on the West Bank must be absorbed at the cost of other needs.[2]

In 1980 Senator Adlai Stevenson introduced legislation to discourage the use of U.S. aid for West Bank settlement. Stevenson did not propose any reduction in aid. Rather, he proposed that $150 million (the then estimated amount spent annually on settlements) be withheld until the President certified that a satisfactory settlement policy was being followed. The Stevenson amendment was defeated by a vote of 85 to 7.

Ian Lustick, Associate Professor of Government at Dartmouth College, and former Council on Foreign Relations Fellow at the State Department, has suggested how the U.S. might give more concrete expression to its opposition to settlements:

> Since 1967, every American Administration has stipulated that no U.S. aid could be used by Israel to fund projects in the occupied territories. This policy has received regular legislative support in Senate and House hearings on annual foreign aid appropriations. Six billion dollars in economic aid have been awarded to Israel between 1967 and 1982, but the ban on the use of our funds beyond the green line [i.e. beyond Israel's 1967 borders — Ed.] has never been enforced. In fact it could not have been, because the aid has been extended under the category of 'security support assistance,' or as it is now labeled, an 'economic support fund.' This kind of economic aid consists of budgetary support in the form of cash transfers (loans and grants) — in contrast to most other aid relationships, the projects we fund in

---

*In March 1980 after voting for a unanimous U.N. Security Council Resolution condemning Israeli settlements, the U.S. announced that there had been a failure in communications and that it should have abstained. Most recently, on August 2, 1983, it cast the negative vote in a 13 to 1 Security Council vote on a resolution critical of the settlements, a resolution supported, among others, by France, the Netherlands, the United Kingdom and the U.S.S.R.

Israel are not specified. Nor has a single official at the State Department or the Agency for International Development (AID) ever been assigned to supervise the use of our funds by the Israeli government.

The transfer of even a small portion of economic assistance to Israel from the 'economic support fund' category to that of 'development assistance' would entail the immediate creation of a bureaucratic mechanism at AID for evaluating and monitoring its use in Israel. For the first time, the ban on Israel's use of U.S. aid beyond the green line could be at least partially enforced.[3]

Now along comes Ian Lustick, associate professor of government at Dartmouth College and author of *Arabs In The Jewish State*, with a radical programme for American action on the West Bank, which is much too sensible to be adopted. . . . [M]onitoring American aid [says Lustick] "would be a strong signal to the Arabs and Israelis alike" to show that we care about the West Bank.

JESSE ZEL LURIE, retired editor and publisher of *Hadassah*, the largest Jewish periodical in the world.

The Jerusalem Post, March 30, 1983

The U.S. Congress annually votes aid (administered by the Agency for International Development) to benefit the inhabitants of the occupied territories. Another study conducted by Meron Benvenisti concluded that the thrust of the U.S. effort has been changed by the Israeli authorities through their power to approve or delay specific projects.[5] The study stated that, by withholding approval of programs designed to assist Palestinian economic development and by favoring projects which would otherwise fall within Israeli budgetary responsibility, the Israeli government has promoted Palestinian dependence on Israel, assisted an Israeli policy of "pacification," and freed Israeli funds for Jewish settlement of the West Bank.

On the conflict over West Bank land, the report states:

> The Israeli authorities turn down almost all projects that involve purchasing of tractors, bulldozers or any other earth-moving equipment. This policy may be attributed to an attempt to prevent Palestinians from reclaiming rough or stoney ground otherwise claimed by the Israeli authorities as 'state land' being 'uncultivable'.

Bernard Avishai, author of the forthcoming book, *The Tragedy Of Zionism*, states that the economic problems confronting Israel are partly attributable to having "spent billions of dollars on housing subsidies, most of it in the West Bank". While aid to Israel must be continued, says Professor Avishai, "it should be clear that any new financial program is meant to aid development inside the pre-1967 borders, not for West Bank settlements or false prosperity that enables Likud to stay in power and pursue its annexationist policies in the territories."[4]

Senator Charles McC. Mathias, Jr., a member of the Senate Foreign Relations Committee, has voiced a U.S. imperative. While emphasizing the need of the Arab world to recognize Israel, Mathias says that the United States administration "should move quickly to sweep aside any doubts in the minds of the new Israeli leadership about the sincerity of the United States opposition to Israel's settlement policy."[6]

FOOTNOTES

1   Message to Middle East Conference, sponsored by *New Outlook*, Washington, D.C., October 25, 1979.

2   *U.S. Assistance To The State Of Israel*, Report by the Comptroller General of the United States, June 24, 1983, p. 28.

3   Ian Lustick, "Israeli Politics And American Foreign Policy," *Foreign Affairs*, Winter 1982-83.

4   Bernard Avishai, "Israeli Economic Ills, *The New York Times*, September 22, 1983.

5   *U.S. Government Funded Projects in the West Bank and Gaza 1977-1983*, The West Bank Data Base Project, Jerusalem, 1984.

6   Address, "Toward Peace In The Middle East," at the Conference On The Search For Peace In The Middle East, Washington, D.C., October 14, 1983.

VIII. *Conclusion*

THE JEWISH PEOPLE have finally achieved the state for which they have for so long yearned. The Palestinians have the same aspirations—a flag, passport, control over their own institutions, self-determination in the land on which they have lived for generations. As expressed in an editorial in *The New York Times:*

> [Palestinian] nationalism, born with the creation of Israel, is a force apart from Soviet rockets and Marxist ideology. Yet unless satisfied at last, it will become ever more radical, threatening to America's Arab friends and burdensome for Israel.
>
> The Palestinians deserve a homeland that, like Israel, will be a beacon to a scattered people even if it cannot absorb them all. The West Bank and Gaza are the only available foundation for that home. . . .[1]

In September 1977 Ann Lesch, former Middle East representative of the American Friends Service Committee, speaking before the U.S. Congress, testified:

> The issue of settlements is not just a matter of dry statistics—numbers of settlements and pinpoints on a map—for either Israelis or Palestinians. Both peoples ascribe a deep emotional significance to the Land. Both view it as their historic patrimony. The Israelis have been able to build a state on part of that land, on which they can develop their culture, economy and society, and in which they can gather Jews from the Diaspora. But the West Bank and Gaza are virtually all that remain to the Palestinians of their patrimony, and they watch it being not only ruled by a foreign power but also being encroached on and taken away from them. Palestinian society on the West Bank and Gaza has its distinctive literature, art, music, customs, and national aspirations. The challenge from Israeli settlements is a challenge to all of their aspirations, and is bitterly resented.[2]

Lesch's comments focused on the impact of settlements on Palestinian aspirations. In February 1984 Larry L. Fabian, Secretary of the Carnegie Endowment for International Peace, and former Director of its Middle East Program, addressed their far more serious impact on peace:

> The point of no return is fast approaching; that much is sure. The closer it gets, the more the trends on the West Bank make a mockery not only of the Camp David formula but of the Reagan Plan or of any other blueprint

149

purporting to promise an end to Israeli control. They make a mockery of claims that Israel is settling the West Bank because it wants to encourage the Arabs to negotiate, or that Israel is planting new settlements for security reasons. They make a mockery of the declared platform of Israel's opposition Labor Party and that of Israel's small but vocal peace movement, both of which profess to offer West Bank compromise as a realistic security and political option, or as a moral imperative. They make a mockery, as well, of the hopes of all those supporters of Israel in the United States who genuinely want to believe that a peaceful future for Israel based on an accommodation with the Palestinians and the Jordanians is still achievable.[3]

In 1982 three prominent international Jews, Nahum Goldmann, Philip M. Klutznick, President Emeritus of the World Jewish Congress, and former Prime Minister of France Pierre Mendez-France called for "mutual recognition between Israel and the Palestinian people . . . based on self-determination."[4] Jacobo Timerman, the renowned journalist has observed:

> Nothing can replace the need of a people to organize into a state in the territory in which they live and which belongs to them. The alternative our [Israeli] government offers, no matter how it masks it, is to continue repressing the Palestinian people until we destroy their will to live and liquidate their national identity. It's incredible that such a policy is being considered by the very people who demonstrated that this is impossible, that it is immoral, that it is criminal.[5]

In 1962 after many years of bitter struggle, France decided to withdraw from Algeria. With the departure of one million French from North Africa, France and Algeria now enjoy peace and peaceful relations. Orthodox scholar and Israeli Professor of Philosophy Yeshayahu Leibowitz drew a parallel:

> Israel must be 'liberated' from the occupied territories as France in the early 1960s had to be 'liberated from the yoke and burden of Algeria.' Israel must be liberated from the territories — or it will perish.[6]

The West Bank must be permitted to retain its Palestinian-Arab character so that it may serve as a Palestinian homeland. Israel, by continuing its settlements and altering the character of the West Bank, seriously jeopardizes the possibility for a just peace in the region.[7] The U.S., by its substantial unqualified financial assistance to Israel, is a party to this unwise policy.

Stephen Rosenfeld, writing in *Present Tense*, a magazine devoted to Jewish issues, calls on American Jews to challenge the Israeli government to freeze the settlements.

> [I]n respect to the Palestinians, the result if not the purpose of [Israeli] policy has been to discourage moderation and thereby to help keep alive the reality of confrontation and the specter of a potentially nuclear war.[8]

Peace Now has issued a similar challenge:

> Because Diaspora Jewry plays such a crucial role in influencing both Israeli public opinion and the actions of the Israeli government, and because the character and destiny of the State of Israel directly affect the entire Jewish people, we believe that Jews in the Diaspora should be able to properly assess the processes now unfolding on the West Bank. Not only is it not unseemly for Diaspora Jews of dissenting opinions to make their voices heard, it is, we believe, the right and duty of every Jew concerned with the Jewish state to confront the political, social and moral implications of occupation, settlement, and annexation.[9]

The New York Times recently reported that Presidential candidate George McGovern received a standing ovation from half the crowd of a largely Jewish audience when he repeated his opposition to the establishment of Israeli settlements on the West Bank and other Israeli policies.[10]

American political leaders who are concerned that questioning Israeli settlement policy be construed as lack of support for Israel can note the sharp shift in sentiment both within Israel and the American Jewish community in the past year. There is substantial evidence that both communities now oppose further settlement (see pp.136,143 above).

Those in Israel and in the American Jewish community with the wisdom and courage to dissent from Israel's destructive policy deserve greater support from Americans. There should be no occasion for an Israeli, because of American indecision, to say "The Americans have totally undermined us."[11]

Israel is dear to Americans for many reasons, not least because it is dear to American Jews. But the conditions on the West Bank are not static; they are deteriorating daily. It is, therefore, imperative that Americans address the issue. Israeli interests, Jewish interests, American interests are all at stake.

FOOTNOTES

1   *The New York Times,* July 11, 1982.

2   "Testimony before the Subcommittees on International Organizations and on Europe and the Middle East of the Committee on International Relations," House of Representatives, September 12, 1977.

3   Larry L. Fabian, "The Middle East: War Dangers And Receding Peace Prospects," *Foreign Affairs,* America And The World 1983.

4   Statement issued in Paris, July 2, 1982. "Today, disagreements among Jews on the questions Klutznick has raised are no longer swept under the rug. They are expressed openly and strongly. For this the American Jewish community owes Philip Klutznick a debt." Estelle Gilson, "Philip Klutznick—Profile of a Gadfly," *Present Tense,* Spring 1984. Klutznick, a former U.S. Secretary of Commerce, argues that peace would permit Israel's economy to grow as much as 50 percent and result in increased immigration to Israel, less emigration and a higher birthrate. With Israel's genius in agriculture, manufacturing and banking, he foresees a role for the country as " the Switzerland" or "the Japan" of the Middle East. *Ibid.*

5   Jacobo Timerman, *The Longest War,* (New York: Alfred A. Knopf, 1982), p. 77.

6   "Outspoken Scholar," *The Jerusalem Post,* September 11, 1981.

7   Meron Benvenisti has concluded that the Israeli expansionists have already won, that "the whole political discussion, which is based on the premise that things are reversible, is irrelevant, and has been overtaken by events," and that the conflict has become an "internal, ethnic" struggle between "superiors and inferiors". Benvenisti, *The West Bank Data Project, supra,* p. x. He believes that holding to the fiction of a "temporary" military occupation is a convenience for the positions of the U.S. and Israeli hawks and doves alike. Benvenisti has produced an impressive study. The West Bank population is, however, still 97 percent Palestinian. Benvenisti acknowledges that "the Palestinians have formed themselves into a solid mass that will not disintegrate" and that the "enlightened world" will not "reconcile itself to the disappearance of the Palestinian nation." *Ibid.,* p. 68. Benvenisti's view of the permanency of Israeli control of the West Bank simply is not acceptable, as the consequences are too serious.

8   Stephen Rosenfeld, "Which Freeze?", *Present Tense,* Summer 1983.

9   *Everything You Didn't Want To Know, supra.*

10 Joyce, "McGovern Stands Apart," *supra.*

11 *Christian Science Monitor,* August 15, 1983.

Appendix A

STATEMENT OF THE LEGAL ADVISER, DEPARTMENT OF STATE, CONCERNING LEGALITY OF SETTLEMENTS IN THE OCCUPIED TERRITORIES, APRIL 28, 1978

THE LEGAL ADVISER
DEPARTMENT OF STATE
WASHINGTON

April 21, 1978

Dear Chairmen Fraser and Hamilton:

Secretary Vance has asked me to reply to your request for a statement of legal considerations underly-
ing the United States view that the establishment of
the Israeli civilian settlements in the territories
occupied by Israel is inconsistent with international
law. Accordingly, I am providing the following in response to that request:

The Territories Involved

The Sinai Peninsula, Gaza, the West Bank and the
Golan Heights were ruled by the Ottoman Empire before
World War I. Following World War I, Sinai was part
of Egypt; the Gaza Strip and the West Bank (as well as
the area east of the Jordan) were part of the British
Mandate for Palestine; and the Golan Heights were part
of the French Mandate for Syria. Syria and Jordan
later became independent. The West Bank and Gaza continued under British Mandate until May, 1948.

The Honorable
  Donald M. Fraser, Chairman
    Subcommittee on International
      Organizations,
        Committee on International Relations
          House of Representatives.

The Honorable
  Lee H. Hamilton, Chairman
    Subcommittee on Europe and the
      Middle East,
        Committee on International Relations,
          House of Representatives.

153

In 1947, the United Nations recommended a plan of partition, never effectuated, that allocated some territory to a Jewish state and other territory (including the West Bank and Gaza) to an Arab state. On May 14, 1948, immediately prior to British termination of the Mandate, a provisional government of Israel proclaimed the establishment of a Jewish state in the areas allocated to it under the partition plan. The Arab League rejected partition and commenced hostilities. When the hostilities ceased, Egypt occupied Gaza, and Jordan occupied the West Bank. These territorial lines of demarcation were incorporated, with minor changes, in the armistice agreements concluded in 1949. The armistice agreements expressly denied political significance to the new lines, but they were de facto boundaries until June, 1967.

During the June, 1967 war, Israeli forces occupied Gaza, the Sinai Peninsula, the West Bank and the Golan Heights. Egypt regained some territory in Sinai during the October, 1973 war and in subsequent disengagement agreements, but Israeli control of the other occupied territories was not affected, except for minor changes on the Golan Heights through a disengagement agreement with Syria.

The Settlements

Some seventy-five Israeli settlements have been established in the above territories (excluding military camps on the West Bank into which small groups of civilians have recently moved). Israel established its first settlements in the occupied territories in 1967 as para-military "nahals". A number of "nahals" have become civilian settlements as they have become economically viable.

Israel began establishing civilian settlements in 1968. Civilian settlements are supported by the government, and also by non-governmental settlement movements affiliated in most cases with political parties. Most are reportedly built on public lands outside the boundaries of any municipality, but some are built on private or municipal lands expropriated for the purpose.

Legal Considerations

1. As noted above, Israeli armed forces entered Gaza, the West Bank, Sinai and the Golan Heights in June, 1967, in the course of an armed conflict. Those areas had not previously been part of Israel's sovereign territory nor otherwise under its administration. By reason of such entry of its armed forces, Israel established control and began to exercise authority over these territories; and under international law, Israel thus became a belligerent occupant of these territories.

Territory coming under the control of a belligerent occupant does not thereby become its sovereign territory. International law confers upon the occupying state authority to undertake interim military administration over the territory and its inhabitants; that authority is not unlimited. The governing rules are designed to permit pursuit of its military needs by the occupying power, to protect the security of the occupying forces, to provide for orderly government, to protect the rights and interests of the inhabitants and to reserve questions of territorial change and sovereignty to a later stage when the war is ended. See L. Oppenheim, 2 International Law 432-438 (7th ed., H. Lauterpacht ed., 1952); E. Feilchenfeld, The International Economic Law of Belligerent Occupation 4-5, 11-12, 15-17, 87 (1942); M. McDougal & F. Feliciano, Law and Minimum World Public Order 734-46, 751-7 (1961); Regulations annexed to the 1907 Hague Convention on the Laws and Customs of War on Land, Articles 42-56, 1 Bevans 643; Department of the Army, The Law of Land Warfare, Chapter 6 (1956) (FM-27-10).

> In positive terms, and broadly stated, the Occupant's powers are (1) to continue orderly government, (2) to exercise control over and utilize the resources of the country so far as necessary for that purpose and to meet his own military needs. He may thus, under the latter head, apply its resources to his own military objects, claim services from the inhabitants, use, requisition, seize or destroy their property, within the limits of what is required for the army of occupation and the needs of the local population.

But beyond the limits of quality, quantum and
duration thus implied, the Occupant's acts will
not have legal effect, although they may in fact
be unchallengeable until the territory is liberated. He is not entitled to treat the country as
his own territory or its inhabitants as his own
subjects,...and over a wide range of public property, he can confer rights only as against himself, and within his own limited period of de
facto rule. J. Stone, Legal Controls of International Conflict, 697 (1959).

On the basis of the available information, the civilian settlements in the territories occupied by Israel
do not appear to be consistent with these limits on Israel's
authority as belligerent occupant in that they do not seem
intended to be of limited duration or established to provide orderly government of the territories and, though
some may serve incidental security purposes, they do not
appear to be required to meet military needs during the
occupation.

2. Article 49 of the Fourth Geneva Convention relative to the Protection of Civilian Persons in Time of War,
August 12, 1949, 6 UST 3516, provides, in paragraph 6:

The Occupying Power shall not deport or transfer parts of its own civilian population into
the territory it occupies.

Paragraph 6 appears to apply by its terms to any
transfer by an occupying power of parts of its civilian
population, whatever the objective and whether involun-
tary or voluntary.* It seems clearly to reach such in-
volvements of the occupying power as determining the lo-
cation of settlements, making land available and financ-
ing of settlements, as well as other kinds of assistance
and participation in their creation. And the paragraph

---

*Paragraph 1 of Article 49, prohibits "forcible"
transfers of protected persons out of occupied territory;
paragraph 6 is not so limited.

appears applicable whether or not harm is done by a particular transfer. The language and history of the provision lead to the conclusion that transfers of a belligerent occupant's civilian population into occupied territory are broadly proscribed as beyond the scope of interim military administration.

The view has been advanced that a transfer is prohibited under paragraph 6 only to the extent that it involves the displacement of the local population. Although one respected authority, Lauterpacht, evidently took this view, it is otherwise unsupported in the literature, in the rules of international law or in the language and negotiating history of the Convention, and it clearly seems not correct. Displacement of protected persons is dealt with separately in the Convention and paragraph 6 would be redundant if limited to cases of displacement. Another view of paragraph 6 is that it is directed against mass population transfers such as occurred in World War II for political, racial or colonization ends; but there is no apparent support or reason for limiting its application to such cases.

The Israeli civilian settlements thus appear to constitute a "transfer of parts of its own civilian population into the territory it occupies" within the scope of paragraph 6.

3. Under Article 6 of the Fourth Geneva Convention, paragraph 6 of Article 49 would cease to be applicable to Israel in the territories occupied by it if and when it discontinues the exercise of governmental functions in those territories. The laws of belligerent occupation generally would continue to apply with respect to particular occupied territory until Israel leaves it or the war ends between Israel and its neighbors concerned with the particular territory. The war can end in many ways, including by express agreement or by de facto acceptance of the status quo by the belligerents.

4. It has been suggested that the principles of belligerent occupation, including Article 49, paragraph 6, of the Fourth Geneva Convention, may not apply in the

West Bank and Gaza because Jordan and Egypt were not
the respective legitimate sovereigns of these territories. However, those principles appear applicable whether or not Jordan and Egypt possessed legitimate sovereign rights in respect of those territories. Protecting the reversionary interest of an ousted sovereign is
not their sole or essential purpose; the paramount purposes are protecting the civilian population of an occupied territory and reserving permanent territorial changes,
if any, until settlement of the conflict. The Fourth
Geneva Convention, to which Israel, Egypt and Jordan are
parties, binds signatories with respect to their territories and the territory of other contracting parties, and
"in all circumstances" (Article 1), in "all cases" of
armed conflict among them (Article 2) and with respect to
all persons who "in any manner whatsoever" find themselves
under the control of a party of which they are not nation-
als (Article 4).

Conclusion

    While Israel may undertake, in the occupied terri-
tories, actions necessary to meet its military needs and
to provide for orderly government during the occupation,
for the reasons indicated above the establishment of the
civilian settlements in those territories is inconsistent
with international law.

                        Very truly yours,

                        Herbert J. Hansell

                        Herbert J. Hansell

Appendix B

**UNITED NATIONS SECURITY COUNCIL RESOLUTION 242
CONCERNING PRINCIPLES FOR A JUST AND LASTING
PEACE IN THE MIDDLE EAST, NOVEMBER 22, 1967**

The Security Council,

Expressing its continuing concern with the grave situation in the Middle East,

Emphasizing the inadmissibility of the acquisition of territory by war and the need to work for a just and lasting peace in which every State in the area can live in security,

Emphasizing further that all Member States in their acceptance of the Charter of the United Nations have undertaken a commitment to act in accordance with Article 2 of the Charter,

1. *Affirms* that the fulfilment of Charter principles requires the establishment of a just and lasting peace in the Middle East which should include the application of both the following principles:

(i) Withdrawal of Israel armed forces from territories occupied in the recent conflict;

(ii) Termination of all claims or states of belligerency and *respect* for and acknowledgement of the sovereignty, territorial integrity and political independence of every State in the area and their right to live in peace within secure and recognized boundaries free from threats or acts of force;

2. *Affirms further* the necessity

(*a*) For guaranteeing freedom of navigation through international waterways in the area;

(*b*) For achieving a just settlement of the refugee problem;

(*c*) For guaranteeing the territorial inviolability and political independence of every State in the area, through measures including the establishment of demilitarized zones;

3. *Requests* the Secretary-General to designate a Special Representative to proceed to the Middle East to establish and maintain contacts with the States concerned in order to promote agreement and assist efforts to achieve a peaceful and accepted settlement in accordance with the provisions and principles in this resolution;

4. *Requests* the Secretary-General to report to the Security Council on the progress of the efforts of the Special Representative as soon as possible.

Appendix C

VIEWS OF THE REAGAN ADMINISTRATION TOWARD ISRAELI SETTLEMENTS IN THE OCCUPIED TERRITORIES

(a) Statement by Secretary of State George P. Shultz to the Foreign Affairs Committee (House of Representatives), September 9, 1982:

Settlements: The status of Israeli settlements must be determined in the course of the final status negotiations. We will not support their continuation as extraterritorial outposts, but neither will we support efforts to deny Jews the opportunity to live in the West Bank and Gaza under the duly constituted governmental authority there, as Arabs live in Israel.

(b) Statement by Ambassador Charles M. Lichenstein, Deputy United States Representative to the United Nations Security Council, August 2, 1983:

We also share the view expressed in the draft resolution that the Hague Regulations of 1907 and the Fourth Geneva Convention of 1949 are applicable to the territories occupied by Israel. The United States Government has stated this position on numerous occasions, and I affirm it again today. Israel, as the occupying power in the West Bank, is bound by the terms of the Fourth Geneva Convention.

Mr. President, the draft resolution contains elements which are unacceptable to the United States, and we, therefore, were obliged to vote against it. Let me make clear, however, that we did not vote against the draft because we approve of Israel's settlement policy. On the contrary, as President Reagan said on September 1, 1982: "further settlement activity is in no way necessary for the security of Israel and only diminishes the confidence of the Arabs that a final outcome can be freely and fairly negotiated.". . .

Appendix D

"STOP THE SETTLEMENTS!" ADVERTISEMENT SIGNED BY ISRAELI PUBLIC FIGURES

The Jerusalem Post (International Edition), July 31-August 6, 1983

A HUNDRED ISRAELI PUBLIC FIGURES, INCLUDING 30 KNESSET MEMBERS, DEMAND:

STOP THE SETTLEMENTS!

We, the undersigned, who differ in our views concerning a solution to the Israeli-Palestinian conflict, are united in regarding the settlement policy of the present Israeli government as dangerous to the security and the future of the State of Israel.

That settlement policy:

- **endangers the security of Israel, contributes to a perpetuation of the conflict and a vicious circle of violence and counter-violence, of suffering, repression and bloodshed;**
- **will frustrate any prospect of arriving at a peaceful solution to the conflict so long as Israel continues to rule over a foreign population and prevents them from realizing their national aspirations;**
- **runs counter to Israel's character as a democratic Jewish State;**
- **diverts resources from vital sectors such as economic development and aid to the underprivileged in development towns, city slums and other depressed areas;**
- **corrupts the soul of the people of Israel, deepens the cleavage within the country and encourages anti-democratic, extremist tendencies;**
- **isolates Israel from the democratic community and alienates the Jews of the Diaspora.**

We call upon the government of Israel to put an end to this ruinous policy, to halt the building of new settlements, to remove this obstacle to the peace process and to encourage negotiations towards a solution which will ensure the security of Israel without negating the rights of other peoples.

Members of Knesset:

Shulamit Aloni	Abba Eban	Hamad Halaila	Haim Ramon	Raphi Souissa
Adi Amorai	Raphi Edri	Aharon Harel	Nachman Raz	Yair Tzaban
Nava Arad	Naftali Feder	Micha Harish	Amnon Rubinstein	Mordechai Virshubski
Uzi Baram	Yaakov Gil	Avraham Katz-Oz	Uri Sabag	Mouhamed Watad
Dov Ben-Meir	Elazar Granot	Aharon Nachmias	Yossi Sarid	Shevah Weiss
Naftali Blumenthal	Menahem Hacohen	Ora Namir	Victor Shemtov	Dov Zakin

Public Figures:

Avraham Adan	Prof. Charles Bloch	David Hacohen	Moshe Mizrachi	Natan Shaham
Yoram Alster	Avraham Burg	Prof. Michael Harsgor	David Moshevitz	Chaim Shur
Levi Argov	Ran Cohen	Prof. Dan Horowitz	Mordechai Nissiyahu	Dr. Arie Simon
Prof. Yehoshua Arieli	Ruth Dayan	Yair Horowitz	Amos Oz	Prof. Uriel Simon
Dr. Janet Aviad	Nissim Eliad	Prof. Assa Kasher	Matti Peled	Amiram Sivan
Dr. Yaakov Arnon	Arie (Lova) Eliav	Prof. Edy Kaufman	Dr. Yoram Peri	Yehoshua Sobol
Yitzhak Auerbuch Orpaz	Prof. Michael Feldman	Dani Karavan	Yehoshua Porat	Prof. Sasson Somekh
Mordechai Bar-On	Dr. Shai Feldman	Zvi Kesse	Amnon Raphael	Yitzhak Taub
Menachem Barabash	Simha Flapan	Moshe Kol	Gideon Raphael	Jesaja Weinberg
Michal Bat-Adam	Yitzhak Frenkel	Prof. Lucien Lazar	Tzali Reshef	Dr. Arieh Yaari
Prof. Shelomo Ben-Ami	Willi Gafny	Yechiel Leket	Shlomo Rosen	Dr. Gadi Yatziv
Ehud Ben-Ezer	Israel Gat	Prof. Shneor Lipson	Yair Rotlevi	A.B. Yehoshua
Naftali Ben-Moshe	Prof. Galia Golan	Prof. Uri Maor	Avraham Schenker	Idit Zertal
Prof. Chaim Ben-Shahar	Dr. Dina Goren	Prof. Avishai Margalit	David Shaham	Dedi Zuker
Yigal Bin-Nun	Chaika Grossman	Nawaf Massalha		

Presented by: **INTERNATIONAL CENTER FOR PEACE IN THE MIDDLE EAST**
107, Hahashmonaim St., Tel-Aviv 67011, Israel, Tel: 03-252285

Appendix E

**LETTER TO PRIME MINISTER MENACHEM BEGIN
FROM AMERICAN JEWISH PUBLIC FIGURES**
Read at a Peace Now rally in Tel Aviv, June 16, 1979

Dear Prime Minister Begin:

We are ardent friends of Israel. We are pledged to a strong and prosperous Israel, and to an Israel at peace with all its neighbors. We have watched with admiration the conclusion of the treaty with Egypt, and we salute the courage and the vision which you brought to that historic achievement.

We are profoundly distressed, however, by the decision of your government to create new settlements on the West Bank. Such a move seems particularly imprudent as critical negotiations on the future of the territories are about to commence. The recent establishment of Elon Moreh impairs Israel's credibility in the eyes of the inhabitants of the West Bank, with whom Israel must find an honorable way to live, and in the eyes of the world. We understand that there are legal and historical arguments for Jewish settlement. But a policy which requires the expropriation of Arab land unrelated to Israel's security needs, and which presumes to occupy permanently a region populated by over 750,000 Palestinian Arabs, we find morally unacceptable, and perilous for the democratic character of the Jewish state.

We are among those who have carried the case for Israel's security to the American people and the American government, and we shall continue to do so. But the present policy on settlements makes our work much more difficult, and the work of the enemies of peace much easier. We appeal to you to reconsider this policy, which only pushes a genuine solution to the Palestinian problem — and, with it, a full and durable peace — still further out of reach.

Respectfully,

Robert B. Alter, Professor, Univ. of California, Berkeley.
Kenneth J. Arrow, Harvard University, Nobel laureate.
Daniel Bell, Harvard University.
Pearl K. Bell, literary critic.
Saul Bellow, writer, Nobel laureate in literature.
Leonard Bernstein, composer and conductor.
Theodore Bikel, actor.
Rabbi Eugene B. Borowitz, Hebrew Union College, Jewish Institute of Religion.
Rabbi Balfour Brickner, Union of American Hebrew Congregations.
Edgar M. Bronfman, chairman, North American Division, World Jewish Congress.
Jacob Cohen, Brandeis University.

Mitchell Cohen, editor, Jewish Frontiers magazine.
Saul B. Cohen, president, Queens College in the City of New York.
Steven P. Cohen, Graduate Center, City University of New York.
Lucy Dawidowicz, historian.
Alan M. Dershowitz, Harvard University.
Amram Ducovny, vice president, Brandeis University.
Leonard Fein, editor, Moment magazine.
Franklin M. Fisher, Massachusetts Institute of Technology.
Paul A. Freund, Harvard University.
Erwin Glikes, vice president and publisher, Harper and Row.
Rabbi Ben Zion Gold, Hillel Foundation, Harvard University.
Marshall I. Goldman, Wellesley College.
Merle Goldman, Boston University.
Anna Maria Gorini, Massachusetts Institute of Technology.
Irving Howe, author and critic.
Hans Jonas, New School for Social Research.
Alfred Kazin, author and critic.
Rabbi Wolfe Kelman, New York.
Walter Laqueur, historian and political analyst.
Irving M. Levine, American Jewish Committee.
Morris L. Levinson, honorary national chairman, United Jewish Appeal
    and member of board of governors, Jewish Agency.
Rabbi Eugene Lipman, Washington.
Seymour Martin Lipset, Stanford University.
Jesse Lurie, executive editor, Hadassah magazine.
Sydney Morgenbesser, Columbia University.
Alfred H. Moses, vice president, American Jewish Committee.
Jacob Neusner, Brown University.
Samuel Norich, vice president, World Jewish Congress.
William Novak, author.
Michael A. Pelavin, Flint, Mich.
Martin Peretz, editor, The New Republic.
Allan Pollack, World Zionist Organization.
Murray Polner, editor, Present Tense magazine.
Rabbi Joachim Prinz, vice president, World Jewish Congress.
Walter A. Rosenblith, provost, Massachusetts Institute of Technology
Henry Rosofsky, Dean of Arts-Sciences faculty, Harvard University
Rabbi Max Ruttenberg, New York.
Benjamin I. Schwartz, Harvard University.
Erich Segal, novelist.
Arden Shenker, Portland, Ore.
Charles E. Silberman, author.
Frederic T. Sommers, Brandeis University.
Marie Syrkin, author.
Melvin Urofsky, historian of Zionism, Univ. of Virginia.
Rabbi Albert Vorspan, Union of American Hebrew Congregations.
Michael L. Walzer, Harvard University.
Leon Wieseltier, Harvard University.
Jerome B. Wiesner, President, Massachusetts Institute of Technology.

Appendix F

SELECTED STATEMENTS FROM AMERICAN JEWISH ORGANIZATIONS ON THE SETTLEMENTS AND THE CONFLICT

AMERICAN JEWISH COMMITTEE:

"The American Jewish Committee believes that U.N. Security Council Resolution 242 embraced in the Camp David Accords, as applied to the West Bank and Gaza, ought to lead to territorial compromise through negotiations and to full peace between Israel and her neighbors. Moreover, the American Jewish Committee shares the concerns of many Israelis that the continuing and indefinite Israeli administration of the West Bank and Gaza, with governance over the lives of more than a million Arabs who are not citizens of Israel, could in the course of time undermine the democratic and humane principles of the State of Israel.

"The American Jewish Committee believes that in the absence of negotiations concerning the West Bank and Gaza, it may well be that Israel's current settlement policy, if continued, may make withdrawal at a later date no longer a viable option for any Israeli government. . . ."

March 21, 1983

CENTRAL CONFERENCE OF AMERICAN RABBIS:

"While Israel itself must be the judge of its own security needs, these decisions also have a fundamental impact on the moral character of Jewish life and on the democratic nature of the Jewish state. We believe that the legitimate demands of security for Israel can—and must—be reconciled with the dignity, human rights and the right of self-determination of Palestinian Arabs. We, therefore, support the concept of territorial compromise, including a temporary cessation of further settlement activities on the West Bank, with the goal of encouraging Jordanian and Palestinian participation in the peace process."

March 15, 1983

NEW JEWISH AGENDA:

Principles of Peace

We believe that to be successful and lasting, a comprehensive settlement must embody the following principles:

1. The Jewish people's right to national self-determination in the State of Israel.
2. National self-determination for the Palestinian people.

3. Mutual recognition and peaceful relations among Israel, the Arab states, and the Palestinians.

4. Withdrawal by Israel from territories occupied since June 5, 1967.

5. Guarantees for Israeli security with recognized borders and mutually agreed-upon provisions responding to the fears and real security needs of all concerned parties.

Toward These Ends, We Join With Israelis and Others in Calling For:

1. Renunciation by all parties of all violence, including terrorism, as means to achieve their aims.

2. Recognition by the Arab states and the Palestine Liberation Organization (P.L.O.) of the right of the State of Israel to exist within secure and recognized borders.

3. Recognition by the State of Israel of the right of the Palestinians to national self-determination, including the right to the establishment, if they so choose, of an independent and viable Palestinian state in the West Bank and Gaza, existing at peace with Israel.

4. Cessation of further Israeli settlement on the West Bank and Gaza, and an end to the repression of the Palestinians.

5. Direct negotiations between Israel and legitimate representatives of the Palestinian people, including the P.L.O., on the basis of mutual recognition and a commitment to peaceful co-existence.

November 28, 1982

Appendix G

Reprinted from *Dissent*, Fall 1980 with permission of the publisher .

J. L. Talmon

"The Homeland Is in Danger"
An Open Letter to Menahem Begin

Last spring the distinguished Israeli historian Jacob Talmon published in the newspaper Haaretz an "Open Letter to Prime Minister Menahem Begin," criticizing the policies of the government with respect to settlements in the West Bank, expansionist and chauvinistic tendencies, etc. This "Open Letter" attracted attention in Israel because of its fundamental character and because its author could not be accused of narrow partisan concerns. We decided to translate the letter for American readers and gained Professor Talmon's consent. He received the first half of the translation and checked it personally but, alas, the heart condition from which he had suffered for some years became acute and he could not check the second half. Professor Talmon died this summer. His friend Abba Eban has kindly gone over the English version, which follows the original Hebrew text except for the omission of some opening reflections on the role of the historian and a few details local to the Israeli scene.—Eds.

Dear Mr. Prime Minister:

"He hoped that it would bring forth grapes, but it brought forth sour grapes." It is now 33 years after the UN General Assembly's vote to establish a Jewish state and 32 years after the young state's soldiers, in the War of Independence, repulsed the Arab armies that threatened its existence. And it is now 14 years since our unprecedented victory in the Six-Day War, and two years after the historic breakthrough of Sadat's visit to Jerusalem. Yet, today we see that the State of Israel is the "Jew among the nations"—isolated, an outcast without legitimacy in the eyes of its enemies, and a nuisance to its friends: its people divided over the all-decisive existential question, its economy on the brink of ruin. . . .

It seems that the rule of law and order has collapsed and that the government is too feeble and cowardly to implement its own decisions or to withstand the pressures of various interest groups. The government encourages the growth of extraparliamentary groups who defy the state and seek to impose their will upon it by force, bringing the dream of a renewed Jewish statehood to derision. We witness with horror a massive emigration of our nation's citizens, among them many *sabras* [native Israelis]. We are also witnessing the heart-breaking spectacle of the Russian "drop-outs"—redeemed from bondage with help secured from the largest superpower— immigrants who seemed to symbolize a miraculous resurrection of the dead. Among the Arab population, there are signs of an organized rebellion instead of the reconciliation envisaged on the basis of the autonomy plan, which was to supplement our treaty with the largest Arab nation. Hardly less alarming is the rampant assimilation of Jews in the Diaspora, only one generation after the Holocaust. What has produced this deterioration? Our task here is not to examine its immediate causes, but to try to understand its structural foundations.

Between the two world wars, the term "lost generation" was widely used in countries that had fought in the First World War. The term referred to the millions of young men who had fallen in the war, but especially to those who

437

came from the elite, whose casualties—because of the unconventional and destructive method of fighting—were disproportionately high. A great many graduates of Oxford and Cambridge were lost in that bloodbath—and so were many of their equivalents in other nations.

One survivor, former English Prime Minister Harold Macmillan, devotes many heart-rending pages in his memoirs to express his sense of being one of the few survivors out of a large and closely knit fellowship. Contemporaries and historians of the 1920s and 1930s who seek to explain the poor quality and lack of imagination of politicians, the cowardly policy of appeasement, and the inability to halt the great economic crisis attribute all this to the absence of the lost generation.

But this catastrophe was nothing compared to the Holocaust that befell our people during the Second World War, resulting in the elimination of Jewish civilization from Europe. Those who were born and educated there before that catastrophe find it impossible to imagine the Jewish streets of the East and Central European cities that were destroyed, the silence of the *shtetlaçh* of the Pale of Settlement, never again to be broken by the sound of prayers coming from the *Bet Midrash* and the *hadarim*. . . . Silenced are the youth of the Hashomer Hatzair and the Betar who once sat around campfires that are now extinguished. Silenced are the prayers of lamentation, the women's "Don't cast us away when we have become old, when our strength has left us, do not abandon us," during the Days of Awe. Gone forever are the street debates between Zionists and Marxists. Gone are the Jewish girls who once greeted the coming of spring on the eve of Passover. Their strong will to live and their faith in the coming national and social revival were destroyed by suffering, humiliation, endless horror, and, finally, death.

My reader will forgive me for being so cruel as to commit to paper what many know but cannot bring themselves to utter: the melancholy truth that the Zionist national liberation movement achieved its goal at the very moment that it lost its standard-bearers. The winds around Auschwitz and Treblinka carry away the ashes of two million potential citizens of the State of Israel, people imbued with intense and genuine Zionist sentiment and the firmest Jewish roots. We shall never be able to replace them.

Yet, the state's first years counterbalanced some of this loss. They witnessed a great explosion of Jewish energy, intelligence, vigilant tension, and feverish activity. We all were summoned to build new foundations, and to absorb hundreds of thousands of immigrants. But the loss was felt later—once the first exuberance began to subside—about two or three years before the Six-Day War.

The very important result of the Six-Day War victory was that it appeared to many as a compensation for the martyrdom of the Holocaust, as a sign that the nation had heroically overcome its tragedy. Indeed, for many, this victory was a testimony to the great change that had taken place in our people—a people that only yesterday had been led like sheep to the slaughter and was now conquering empires.

Many among the Orthodox had difficulty accepting the Holocaust within the scheme of Providence and Jewish history, for they could not see the death of more than a million innocent Jewish children as punishment for sins of the whole Jewish people. What kind of sin would justify such punishment? They did not like to speak or think about the Holocaust. I remember Zalman Aranne's impassioned cry to the Orthodox representatives in the Knesset: "I will never forgive you for not having produced a second Book of Lamentations after the Holocaust!" After the Six-Day War, therefore, the Orthodox were much relieved, for now they could argue that the Holocaust had been the "birth pangs of the Messiah," that the Six-Day War victory was the Beginning of Redemption, and the conquest of the territories the finger of God at work—all proof that the vision of renewal and God's promises were being fulfilled.

The non-Orthodox nationalists soon caught this fever. A while ago, our Foreign Minister Yitzhak Shamir gave a perfect demonstration of this mentality when he said that our generation was not "entitled" to give up Judea and Samaria and the Gaza Strip—implying that these territories were the heritage of all generations of Jews, past, present, and future. Our generation, singled out to be the trustee of this heritage, does not have the "right" to let these sacred lands slip out of our hands.

Is this an eternal belief that will never falter or waiver? Is it loyalty to an ideal vision that no enemy, no suffering, no catastrophe will ever overcome? Or is this merely the manifestation of a classically Jewish characteristic, which the Jews may have bequeathed to other monotheistic religions—namely the need to subordinate oneself to an idea, to a vision of perfection, to an ascetic and ritualistic way of life—instead of treating life as it really is, as did the Greeks, for example, who perceived reality as a challenge and sought to extract from life and nature all the possibilities inherent in them, in order to expand the mind and give pleasure to both body and soul? In short, is it a compulsive drive that makes us deny our essential human nature? Or is this perhaps the sign of a tragic inability to live with the fact of the Holocaust and the reality it has left us with? Is it our inability to adjust to them and, consequently, a detachment from what Freud called "the reality principle"? Is it an escape into a world of mythological thought patterns and emotions whose classic example may be found in Sabbatianism? What is the meaning of that widespread determination to return to where we were in 1939, and to go from there to the farthest reaches of our emotion, as if the ghastly bloodletting had never taken place and Jewish reality and global realities had remained unchanged?

The extent of our Six-Day War victory encouraged this trend. It made us forget that, in Nietzsche's words, "there are victories that are harder to bear than defeats," and that victory in battle is by no means proof of true and enduring strength, unless it is supported by other components, such as an adequate economic infrastructure, a homogeneous population, appropriate geopolitical factors, favorable world opinion, a network of alliances, political experience, and more. For commitments or aspirations that exceed one's objective ability to carry them out are a trap. Pursuing policies that harm the vital interests of other important states—flying in the face of accepted values, of an age—give rise to an opposition that will undercut such political initiatives.

I have never doubted that we reached a turning point when the government of Israel in the summer or fall of 1967 (right after the Six-Day War) abandoned its declared policy that Israel has no territorial claims and is willing to return all occupied lands in exchange for peace. I regard this disavowal as a fatal error, a denial of the UN resolution on partition arrived at 20 years before that—and of the principle of partition itself. I believe this disavowal reopened the Israeli-Arab conflict, after the family of nations had recognized the solution that was reached as a stable and accepted fact of political life, despite the friction, the incidents of terror, and the general bloodletting. This new policy was a grievous error, and it had no chance of success.

There are some who argue that the Khartoum resolutions closed all the doors to peace. I am not an expert in these matters, but people whose opinion I respect claim that close inspection of these resolutions reveals more flexibility than was generally perceived. It is reasonable to suspect that there were those in the Israeli leadership and public who were relieved when the Khartoum conference created this impression, and when the "telephone call" from Hussein never came. I do not believe that the National Unity government and the Labor Alignment had a Machiavellian determination not to budge and not to give up one inch of captured territory. The majority, in fact, recoiled from the idea of total annexation. Yet, at the same time, it was unable to relinquish the territories for Zionist, political, and strategic reasons. There was also the evidence that our military superiority was unshakable, that the PLO's terror was bearable, that the Arab population was passive, Egypt had broken loose from Russia, Hussein was liquidating the terrorists, the Arab countries were as usual fighting among themselves, and America was not exerting pressure—on the contrary, it was supplying us with great quantities of aid and weapons. So why move?

You never know what can happen in the Middle East, and since politics cannot long endure inactivity or deadlock, and since the indecisive usually let themselves be dragged after the resolute, the government and the moderates had neither the strength nor the conviction to oppose partisan attempts to establish settlements, spontaneously, or with the support of sympathizers inside the government who provided half-hearted assistance or accepted whatever the settlers did as a *fait açompli*, or acted out of electoral considerations.

I remember a meeting initiated by then-Foreign Minister Abba Eban in 1969 between senior professors of the Hebrew University and the leadership of the Ministry of Defense. I was asked to express my opinion. I said that as a historian whose diagnosis, like that of a physician, must not be influenced by personal interests, I did not know of any instance where a conflict as complicated and tinted with emotion, irrationality, fears, and feelings of vengeance was ever solved without the involvement of a superpower, alone or in concert with other powers, to offer advice, mediation, and sometimes to impose a solution. In a talk a few days ago with one of Israel's most talented and important diplomats, we agreed that history would not absolve the United States from the fault of not entering into the arena long before 1973. This should have been its responsibility as the leading superpower of the period.

Despite the usual boast of liberated nations of having achieved freedom solely by their own courage, there is almost no example in history in which a national movement did not require the active aid of at least one great power—whose support flowed from self-interest, or from historic or ideological sentiments. Naturally, support from abroad only comes once the people themselves have risen in revolt and proved their stubborn resistance. The Greeks in the 19th century were perhaps the first to succeed in kindling

world opinion against their enemies by the use of a greath myth. All the bravery and martyrology of the Irish and the Poles, however, did not help them in the 20th century; no great power was prepared to tangle with Britannia, "ruler of the waves," or to risk tampering with the balance of the three great northern powers who regarded the dissection of Poland as basic to their alliances.

In recent years, our status has been that of rebels against the international system. Nothing is easier than to win applause for fulminations against the wicked gentiles, the stupidity and selfishness of the nations. Yet, all these accusations, though not groundless, do not explain our condition or advance our cause.

Every national liberation movement is initially a kind of rebellion against the international order. International law is usually on the side of the states that are in power. It consecrates existing authority and the status quo. Rebels seek to change things, if necessary by force; they try to move borders, to upset the balance of power. But every liberation movement that attains independent statehood expresses—by the very act of joining the family of nations—its willingness to accept the rules of the international game by fulfilling two conditions: a readiness to accept international law and proof of its ability to maintain law and order within its own borders regardless of the nature of the regime.

In the last two or three years, the State of Israel sometimes has given the impression that it is far from scrupulous in its observance of the first condition, and that it is incapable of fulfilling the second. The doctrines proclaimed by Israel's official spokesmen, or by spokesmen in good standing with the government, are directly opposed, or unacceptable, to the family of nations. Situations are created that are reminiscent of the stand of revolutionary France, which, by proclaiming the principle of the people's sovereignty, denied the obligations taken on earlier by the French kings vis-à-vis other kings at a time when they embodied the sovereignty of their states. Yet, France still demanded that the foreign kings' commitments toward France continue as valid obligations, since these other states had not yet liberated themselves from the monarchical yoke.

We claim, similarly, that the West Bank and the Gaza Strip are not conquered territories and that therefore the restrictions of international law do not apply to us, particularly with regard to settlement, confiscation of land, and so forth, since we consider these lands to have been "liberated." This claim, by the way, has a long and respectable history; for the term "occupation" went out of fashion with the French Revolution and every conqueror since has proclaimed himself a "liberator." The extremists in Gush Emunim, on the other hand, use religious sanctions in order to justify their activities in the territories.

There is nothing more contemptible and harmful than the use of religious sanctions in a conflict between nations. It is doubltful whether the young man from Gush Emunim who made the Elon Moreh appeal had any idea of the Pandora's box he was opening when he argued, crudely but in a seemingly honest manner, that he and his comrades wanted to settle in the place they had chosen, not for reasons of security but because God had commanded the Children of Israel to inherit the Land of Canaan. Wars of religion cannot be resolved by compromise, by "give and take a little"; and this young man was provocatively inviting a Muslim declaration of *Jihad* and a Vatican pronouncement that since the Jews had rejected Jesus they were no longer the "chosen people" and thus God's promises to Abraham were now invalid.

A religious claim is valid when it relates to matters between people and their creator—to prayer, fast, atonement, faith, and ritual. It does, however, inspire opposition if it disregards others' claims and assumes the right to impose its way, or to harm the rights, freedoms, and interests of others. A religious claim will give a strong impression of hubris, an ambition of mastery, if it tries to subordinate the believers of one religion to those of another. It is one thing for the believer to remain within the boundaries of debate over passages in his holy books and theological commentaries; it is quite another if behind him stand tanks, planes, missiles, soldiers, and police, ready to use direct or indirect violence.

An influential American journalist told me recently about "a dialogue of the deaf and dumb" he had held with members of Gush Emunim who had attempted to persuade him that theirs was a holy war. The non-Jew pressed them: "What does the use of tanks and planes, the occupation of territories and political rule, have to do with religion?" "Don't you understand," they replied, "for us, religion is total, and religious commandments and political practice are interdependent." This kind of Khomeiniism is likely to return us to the days when millions were ready to join the Crusades to slaughter millions of others in order to keep them from going to Hell, in their own way, and to the early militaristic days of Islam when Holy War was declared against non-believers desecrating the name of God and thereby insulting the believers. This is just like Qaddafi of Libya, who dreams of an Islamic Europe and feels an obligation to aid all, including terrorist anarchists, who seek to shake the foundations of Western civilization.

After hundreds of thousands had been killed, or had died of hunger and plague, and entire nations had been destroyed, Europe grew tired of religious wars. Shrewd people realized that before the believers would have a chance to arrive in Heaven, the zealots on all sides would have turned the earth into Hell. They resolved to separate religion completely from politics, just as they had once separated religion from science. Claims such as those of Gush Emunim sound to the international community much like that biblical passage— "Sun, stand thou still upon Gibeon, and thou, Moon, in the Valley of Ayalon"—would sound in an astronomers' debate.

In the eyes of most of the earth's people— that is to say, the cultures that do not know the Bible, the Covenant made between God and the Jewish people, or even our historic right to the Land of Israel—all this is not binding. The Christian nations, in as much as they still have attachment to the Bible, usually

441

treat the biblical stories (so—we must admit—do most Jews) as allegories produced by primitive tribes who had not yet reached a high level of abstraction.

The term "historic rights" does not connote a *Kushan* (certificate of registration), a term that characterizes the special link between the Jewish people and its unique cultural and religious contribution to civilization—the spiritual bond between generations that connects the dispersed people to its ancient origins. There is also the fact that throughout centuries of wandering, the Jews have been unable—because of historic memories and universal hostility—to strike roots as citizens and, no less important, to create a political entity in any other territory. Therefore, when the age of self-determination had come, this people found itself persecuted, slandered, outcast, and homeless. It surely seemed natural that it would be promised a home, located in the territory with which it was historically identified and where it would live as a normal nation.

But it is a far stretch from this point to the sanctification of political frontiers that have gone through so many changes in the history of all nations and all times. Even in the age of Jewish political rule in the Land of Israel, large portions of the country were either settled by other ethnic groups or controlled by foreign rulers. What place do Acco, Jenin, Halhul, or Gaza have in Jewish history, compared with Toledo, Vilna, Odessa, and Warsaw? No matter how frustrating it might be, we cannot expect the international community, whose guiding principle is the right of every nation and tribe to self-determination, to treat the Arabs of the Land of Israel, the Palestinians, as a group of bandits who have broken into someone else's home while the owner was away, and are now illegal squatters who must leave this place to make room for the returning owners, or settle for the status of second-class tenants with whatever autonomy the owner, now ruler of the land, deigns to grant them.

It is accepted among historians concerned with nationalism that continuity and the creation of a collective way of life are the foundations of nationhood; a historian does not ask who were the first settlers, for most of those have since been lost or have migrated. One might argue that the Palestinians did not develop a collective consciousness, language, culture, or specific political framework of their own; or that neither the great Arab civilization nor humanity in general would lose anything if a twenty-third Arab state was not established. But once the consciousness of a "we" arises in an ethnic group that is in conflict with settlers alien to themselves, those arguments cannot cancel the fact, undesirable as it may be, that there may well occur a head-on collision between two national movements. We have long preferred to disregard this fact.

Mr. Prime Minister, with all due respect to you as head of the government and as a fellow historian, permit me to make an observation, on the basis of decades of study of the history of nationalism. However ancient, special, noble, and unique our subjective motives may be, the desire, at the end of the 20th century, to dominate and govern a hostile foreign population that differs from us in language, history, culture, religion, consciousness, and national aspirations, as well as in its economic and social structure is like an attempt to revive feudalism.

The question is not a moral one. The idea is simply not feasible, nor is its realization worth the price—as France learned in Algeria. The Soviet analogy is irrelevant: we have neither the material strength nor the requisite spiritual and moral toughness. The only way to bring nations to exist together in our day, ironic and disappointing as it is, is by separating them. God Himself, nature, and history divided the Land of Israel before it was ever divided by human decree. It may well be that the most powerful force that can impel individuals, classes, and nations to act in the modern era is the determination to oppose the hereditary humiliation of an inferior position, arising from the subjection of one people by another. Political inequality leads invariably to social and economic inferiority, since the ruling nation, motivated by feelings of tribal solidarity and fear "lest they multiply and

442

become mightier," will try to restrict the growth and power of the subject population, denying it access to office, responsibility, and sensitive positions and, of course, to any activity defined as "subversive." The combination of political subjection, national oppression, and social inferiority is a time bomb. Voltaire is said to have remarked that all men are born equal but that the population of Timbuktu has not yet heard the news.

But by now they have heard the news, and since then the world has not known a moment's peace. Whoever speaks of the need for one people to rule over another for security reasons leads his audience astray. To do so is to sit deliberately on a volcano; it is a source of insecurity and perpetual alarm. The rebellious hostility of a subjected population, particularly if it is supported by millions on the other side of the border, neutralizes any degree of security provided by holding on to this hill or that stream, a strait or marsh, in an age of long-range missiles and bombs. There is something repulsive in the kind of cynicism or naïveté that claims that settlements are needed to create conditions of coexistence, while everyone knows that for the Arabs each settlement is another sign of dispossession and gradual conquest. The Jewish image suffers as a result of such double-talk that does nothing to enhance our security or honor.

The world is not naïve. It does not believe the claim that a few trailers on a rocky mountain will block the path of a modern army or deter it. Historians remember very well what happened to the Maginot Line, the Siegfried Line, and even the Bar-Lev Line, and how the assurances of the war minister of Napoleon III that the French army was "prepared to the last button" were proven false—or claims that this or that natural barrier would save a nation from destruction. This does not mean that bargaining over borders is impermissible, particularly if such a change will not lead to domination over a foreign population more numerous than it was in the age of feudalism. In the modern age, it is not land that is inherited but the consciousness and will of the people living in it.

Any talk of the holiness of the land or of geographic sites throws us back to the age of fetishism. One of the greatest living Orthodox rabbis in America once told me that he does not know of one authentic holy site in the Land of Israel except for the Wailing Wall. "I even have my doubts about the Cave of Machpelah," added this rabbi, who refuses to give any support to political rabbis.

Your concept of autonomy, Mr. Prime Minister, is an anachronism—a device to lull foreign public opinion. Anyone who has taken a look at the history of the multinational empires of the Hapsburgs and the Romanovs at the end of the 19th century will shake his head at this idea exhumed from the historical junk pile. The last word on Otto Bauer's and Karl Renner's Austrian experiment with autonomy was said at Sarajevo—the inauguration of the greatest international catastrophe till that day. The days of autonomies in the frail states that were erected on the ruins of the Czarist empire were short, hard-pressed, and without glory.

The idea of "personal autonomy," which you took over from the Austrian Marxists, was never proposed by them as an end in itself. Its aim was to supplement and realize territorial autonomy. It was intended for ethnic groups living outside their "homeland." Now, if you apply these ideas to our situation, who can guarantee that the Arabs on our side of the Green Line will not also demand "autonomy"—if it is going to be a permanent condition in the territories?

It is hard to believe that any population would agree to this sort of "autonomy," without a legislative assembly of its own, or that such people would settle for a mere "administrative council" subordinate to the executive authority of an alien sovereignty. History abounds with examples of such legislative assemblies ending up by declaring their independence. When this happens here, will we use our soldiers to disband such a legislative assembly, and will we then put its insurgent leaders on trial for treason?

Let us keep in mind that those who designed this sort of "autonomy" for the national minorities of the Austro-Hungarian Empire argued, and some believed, that the

443

empire's territory was not the sole possession of the dominant nationality—but that it belonged equally to all the ethnic and national groups that lived within its boundaries. And let us keep in mind that this belief engendered strong opposition to the recognition of one dominant language (German) or even of a *Verkehrssprache* in the Austro-Hungarian Empire. This notion stood in sharp contrast to the concept of an "autonomy" that is graciously granted to minorities by the sovereign people—a people that conceives of itself as the sole sovereign. In our case, we are speaking of a sovereign people that holds on tightly to the ownership of land, to sources of water, to rights to unrestricted settlement— while permitting the national groups to which it has graciously given "autonomy" the right to care for the sewers, to immunize their children, and to maintain elementary schools while unable to determine the content or spirit of what is taught in those schools.

Giving a minority autonomy makes sense— if it is intended as an interim solution for a specified length of time and as a chance to find out if the two nationalities in question can pass the test of coexistence, and can live together as neighbors, in peace.

There are those who say, "But our vital security interests make it imperative that we hold on to our sovereignty over *all* of the present territories of the Land of Israel; and settlements in the territories are crucially needed for our defense." We have already heard from two of your ministers of defense and from some generals that this just is not the case. Such claims (as the thinking majority of the country has known all along) are mere rationalizations for the pursuit of other goals. On the contrary, these settlements are at present destructive of our vital interests and of our Zionist goals—and especially of peace with our neighbors, which is the precondition for achieving all other goals.

To focus solely on the dangers to security arising from the loss of the territories is a grave demagogic error. It sounds strange indeed when it comes, as it usually does, from those who never tire of repeating what a big power we are, and how we are the only secure bastion of the U.S. and of the entire West in the Middle East.

If we are so vulnerable that our entire security depends on a few kilometers of barren hills, what kind of bastion can we possibly be to anyone? This argument from "security" surely must raise doubts in our allies' minds as to our ability to survive at all; and it must make them wonder if it is indeed worthwhile to give us the aid we are constantly requesting in order to guarantee our security. When an Israeli minister and a former general [Arik Sharon] rebukes the American Jewish leadership for keeping silent during the Holocaust, he creates panic lest Israel is on the brink of destruction. Such foolish remarks make it easier for American Jews to understand why Russian immigrants are leaving Israel, and why so many Israelis, too, are emigrating to the U.S. So, for all the noise and tumult surrounding the settlements issue, who, really, are the defeatists—and who are the "brave patriots" who know no fear?

Israel, obviously, is surrounded by enemies prepared to drown it in a sea of blood. Yet, has not Sadat given proof that there are other Arabs, too, who for one reason or another are ready to accept our existence? This now is a fact—for whatever reason. Perhaps it is because such Arabs have concluded that they cannot annihilate us by force, and perhaps because they hope that the State of Israel will destroy itself through its own internal contradictions and its economic weakness, and perhaps because of apathy among Jews in the Diaspora.

It is indeed dangerous to argue that the State of Israel is incapable of defending itself without holding onto the captured territories (granted, of course, some minor rectification of some borders will have to be made for authentic reasons of security). For this implies that Israel cannot exist at all. Is the River Jordan as wide as the Volga or the Mississippi? Are the mountains of Nablus as high as the Himalayas? Does anyone remember the slogan that Sharm el-Sheikh without peace is better than peace without Sharm el-Sheikh? Let us face it, Mr. Prime Minister, the real danger to the existence of the State of Israel lies in continuing the Sisyphean attempt to defeat the Palestinians: whoever cannot see now the grave threat of a binational war is blind.

Those of us who speak out against the settlements are opposed by your supporters who ask, "Is not settlement the life-blood of Zionism? What is the difference between Degania in 1913 and Eilon Moreh in 1980? If we don't have the right to settle now, then what gave us the right to do it then?" In considering these arguments, we should remember that history is a record of change. History does not stand still or repeat itself exactly; it is the record of interrelationship and objective change—and the presence (or lack) of human wisdom. Loyalty to a historic tradition is not expressed in a neurotic dependence on past models. It is expressed in frank acknowledgment, with the necessary flexibility, of new and unexpected situations, while preserving the essential core of that tradition, which may take different forms at different times.

History's fuel is not to be found in abstract ideas or utopian desires for adventurism, or in romanticism—but in brutal force that cannot be withstood. Without this force the caravans of history would not be on the move. And if the enthusiasm of the avant-garde succeeds in moving it a bit, it will be stopped when the power runs out. Who has not heard of revolutions or uprisings that were attempted too soon or too late, before or after a change in the supporting factors inherent in a revolutionary condition, in a crisis, or in a particular international constellation?

And here we all remember Marx's poignant remark that history has a compulsion to repeat itself—in situations that may seem similar but are in reality radically different. "History repeats itself, the first time as tragedy, the second time as farce." This remark is now relevant to the present analogy that compares "the towers and the stockades" in the Galilee of our founding days with the improvised colonization of today. But our modern activists are not the pioneers who built roads where there were none, who outmaneuvered cruel enemies and avoided the danger of annihilation. Today's settlers in

the territories rely on our army's tanks, helicopters, and planes. They come to demonstrate our presence, to display our force—*not* to plow, to sow, or plant. These settlements are more than a desperate attempt to hold onto the territory of our homeland. They are a political act and its principal purpose is to determine who will rule or, as the settlers put it, "to show the Arabs who is the boss here. . . . to put the Arabs in their place."

Such settling, it seems to me, is tantamount to conducting a kind of war. It will be very difficult to prevent the situation from turning into a head-on collision between two peoples in a land that suffers from "agrarian famine." This process resembles the agrarian wars in Ireland, between colonizing English noblemen and Irish tenant farmers, or Prussia's policy concerning the Polish peasantry within its territory. It is the same wretched discrimination, extortion, robbery, fraud, and repression, on the one hand—and agrarian rebellion and military repression, on the other hand. It is an unfair struggle between two nations when one side can rely on military power, and the other must hold on with its bare teeth and fingernails to its impoverished, tired, arid land. The same holds true when we contemplate the struggle against a foreign invader and a repressive regime. Who is not ashamed when confronted with the wretched sight of Bedouins being driven out, having to move on, again and again, from place to place—"for famine was in the land, and there was no pasture for the sheep. . ."? And all this is done in the name of preserving the nation's laws—as if the Bedouins were accustomed to living in Holland or Switzerland, as a brutal and arrogant general once said.

For all the shame and pain we feel over the harm done to us by our neighbors because of anachronistic perverse policies, our fear should be greater over what these acts will do to us, to the Jewish people, and to our dream of social and moral justice and renaissance. For this dream was one of the vital and beautiful aspects of Zionism, setting it apart from other national liberation movements. The desire to dominate, Mr. Prime Minister, leads to perpetual fear and mistrust of the subjugated people and creates terrible temptations that are stronger than any subjectively good intentions.

This situation of perpetual terror and counterterror, retaliatory raids and protective strikes unleashes aggressive and evil impulses that the rule of law barely manages to control. In such an atmosphere nothing positive can develop, there can be no vitality, no joy in living. Do you remember Jean Jaurès' famous answer at the time of the Dreyfus affair to those who saw no reason for socialists trying to save a bourgeois officer from other bourgeois officers? "If we allow evil and aggression and violence to run wild," said Jaurès, "then the whole earth will be corrupted, until it will no longer be fit for socialism." Now, in our country, such corruption is no longer a masochist's bad dream; it is a reality, and it is strangling us. And this is not the product of a government that enjoys tyranny for its own sake—but of a weak government that pretends to be strong and is forced to camouflage its weakness with trickery. This weakness is promoted by zealots who have lost all sanity and common sense and who receive their funding at the expense of tens of thousands of young people living in poverty, all because everything is dedicated to the pipedream that the settlements will be able to prevent the establishment of a PLO state and stave off the opposition of world opinion.

Could the settlements really prevent the establishment of a PLO state—and how are they to assuage world opinion?

Most of our people either oppose or have strong reservations about the settlements. Needless to say, world public opinion universally denounces the current policy as a violation of international law and, indeed, as a unilateral provocation that makes the idea of negotiation seem ridiculous. From this follows the conspiratorial pattern in which these settlements are established, and the way they are fenced in, "for military purposes." The seizure or purchase of land, "for public use," proceeds much in the same way. This is not the way a sovereign, law-abiding nation

should operate, nor is it the way of a society whose openness, until now, has always been one of its most admirable qualities.

So it has happened that a government whose leaders were reared on slogans of Jewish pride and honor is now turning our state into an underground movement, using arguments and excuses so blatantly deceitful that they inevitably conjure up in the gentile imagination the figures of the contemptible scheming Jews of traditional anti-Semitic folklore. One of your [former] cabinet ministers [Ezer Weizman], Mr. Prime Minister, has already publicly commented that "we are succeeding in making ourselves hateful to the whole world."

Since the government, for one reason or another, is unable or afraid to initiate its own settlement policy, an avant-garde of passionate zealots has emerged that proclaims itself the protector of the national destiny. These people consider themselves destined to operate in the territories without regard for a cowardly government or for our laws. For these zealots believe that our courts have no jurisdiction when it comes to faith. Indeed, these zealots consider anyone who opposes them as nothing less than traitors.

The result is contempt for the courts; disregard for governmental decrees; scorn for the rule of law and the rights of others—in short, wanton lawlessness in the guise of ardent patriotism. All this is happening while this movement's fifth column within the government succeeds in suppressing the voices of opponents. This century has suffered much, and the Jewish people more than most, from similar groups of a "nation's finest," which always claim they are saving their country, in the name of a divine sanction that allows them proudly to trample on the laws of a democratic society and on human morality.

And so these zealots speak of "the need of the hour," in order to whip up nationalist feelings and to exploit sources of religious mysticism—to fight, in the spirit of the old-time Zealots against any form of wicked "Hellenization." And so they aim to suppress the spirit of pluralism and of skepticism, and to strangle any crticism at home or abroad. In short, our latter-day zealots are determined to adopt the doctrines of integralist nationalism whose French prophet, Maurice Barrès, once defined truth as the angle of sight of the French national interest. The same imperialistic brand of nationalism flooded Europe at the beginning of the 19th century, and everywhere it made hatred of the Jews its emblem.

Instead of being a nation that is experiencing a renaissance, a nation that is courageous, and proud to be a member of the family of nations, we are manifestly returning to a mentality and a system of actions that rather befit an isolated and Diaspora-bound religious sect. Is it not the way of a sect to remain insistently on the margins of history and to isolate itself from the world? Such a sect, however, is also capable of becoming an armed band of guerrillas, fighting with the instruments of modern technology—according to the patterns of a well-known Master Race.

The Romantic movement of the 19th century gave rise to modern Zionism and the modern idea of a national revival of the Jewish people. The goal of a return to Zion, of course, had been alive among the Jewish people ever since our exile from the Land of Israel. It sustained us through centuries of dispersion. Over the centuries and throughout the Diaspora, Jews have prayed, and still pray, for this return, night and day.

Modern Zionism was one of the last movements to espouse national liberation. It flowered late in the tremendous wave of movements that fought for national freedom after the French Revolution. Almost every suppressed people then began to struggle for liberation—from the Eskimos to the natives of Papua, from the Basques to the tribes of Baluchistan. The driving force behind these movements was, and still is, the concept of human dignity, and of the right of every ethnic or national group to freedom and self-expression. This aspiration captured the imagination of the subjugated nations. And so the search for identity and the desire to express it led national groups to an exploration of their roots. Many began to make a cult of their past, for this was how they could

emphasize their uniqueness. Such heralds and prophets of political nationalism as Moses Hess, Leo Pinsker, Theodor Herzl, Max Nordau, and even Ze'ev [V.] Jabotinsky did not draw their inspiration from religious experience or even from Jewish history; at least, not in the beginning. They were stirred by the concept of human dignity. They wanted to heal the injuries to Jewish pride, and yearned for the Jewish people hereafter to be spared all humiliation and persecution; it was their burning desire to see the Jewish people in freedom—a member of the family of free nations. These early Zionist leaders were moved to take a more active role in Jewish life by this general awakening of interest in ethnic roots, dignity, and liberation. Even the Zionism of Rabbi Kalischer and Rabbi Alkalai was aroused by the wars of liberation that were being fought by the Greeks, the Serbs, the Hungarians, the Romanians, and the Bulgarians. Moses Hess was inspired by the vision of the resurrection of Athens and of Rome—which he believed to herald, inevitably, the resurrection of Jerusalem.

The Jews were, so to speak, the "last to arrive at the feast" among the movements of national liberation. During the "Spring of Nations" of 1848, the Jews were the only national or ethnic group that did not experience a national awakening. The Jews, however, enthusiastically greeted the revolution as a victory for the ideal of the brotherhood of nations. Many emancipated Jews saw the revolution as a sign that the hour had now come for the Jews to give up their unique status of "chosenness." But then, around 1880, there rose up a murderous wave of mass anti-Semitism—ironically, just at the moment when it seemed as if the dream of human rights had triumphed throughout the world. This fearful wave of anti-Semitism deeply shocked the sensitive, assimilated, European Jews.

At this very time, in Eastern Europe, after the liberation of the serfs, millions of impoverished peasants and aristocrats flowed into the Jewish towns and cities. Thus the Jews faced a situation of danger precisely when their religious security had substantially weakened and their snobbish feelings of cultural and intellectual superiority over their "boorish neighbors" were on the rise. The combination of these two trends moved hundreds of thousands of young Jews to join the revolutionary, or nationalist, movements—or to leave their homes and emigrate to America.

This is not to say that Zionism lacked faith in God's promises, and in the hope of redemption, or that it did not derive sustenance from prayers that speak of the return to the land of our fathers; but these were not the sparks that lit the great fires of political Zionism. On the contrary, it was the Jewish people's religious life that received new sustenance through these Zionist, and political, developments. It is quite reasonable to claim that the Jewish religion actually prevented the vision of redemption from being turned into a historical and political concept. The Jewish religion served as a substitute for redemption; the reliance on Providence, on the Messiah, and on miracles, exempted Jews from acting in the here and now. The religion, in a way, even prohibited them from doing so, for the law could be observed and the feelings of longing expressed anywhere in the world . . . and is not today's enthusiastic Zionism-by-proxy of millions of Jews in the Diaspora proof of this? It is no coincidence that Jewish orthodoxy was from the first suspicious of and even hostile to Zionism. Like the Catholic Church, it viewed nationalism as a serious secular competitor to religion and, to a certain extent, as the sin of hastening redemption, without waiting for the Messiah.

Some people argue that it was not solely an internal dialectic—but rather the persecution of the Jews that was the principal reason for the rise of Zionism and for the sympathy extended to it by the best of the gentiles. These people, indeed, are saying something that is elementary to the historian: no matter how great the power of ideas or ideology in the shaping of history may be, the progress of history in the end is determined by various forces, and by various kinds of distress. It is enough, for example, to recall the periodic ebb and flow in the movements of immigra-

tion into the Land of Israel in order to demonstrate that this is so. Let us compare, for instance, the wave of immigration in the 1920s with the huge waves of emigration today, during Israel's statehood.

Mr. Prime Minister, you should not regard these meditations as an attempt to defend the creation of a Palestinian or a PLO state. I am not concerned here with the rights of the Arabs regarding whose past and culture I have little knowledge or interest. I am concerned with Israel's security and welfare. And I am concerned with the quality of the people and culture that make up Israel. I have no doubt that the attempt to rule a million and a quarter Arabs against their will may result in corruption and make our beautiful dreams of national and spiritual renewal seem ridiculous. I am convinced that the annexation of the territories will not only fail to increase our security but will also weaken our ability to defend ourselves against hostile neighbors and international opposition.

In a debate with Arnold Toynbee, right after the Six-Day War, I spoke in favor of what later became known as the "Jordanian orientation." I do tremble at the thought of flag-waving PLO brigades streaming into the occupied territories, firm in their belief that they are taking only the first step toward the complete destruction of the State of Israel. . . . Is it possible that our intransigence could destroy any chance—as it has done in the past, when we were in a position of real strength—of accepting another possible kind of settlement, such as an agreement with Jordan, on the basis of partition?

There will be no alternative to a PLO state, if we continue systematically to ignore the Jordanian option, or other possibilities that many seem to fear more than a PLO victory. Nor will we find salvation in an "information" campaign, which solely consists of denunciations of the PLO as Nazis—if we do not put forward a constructive plan that is based on reasonable compromise. Our generation can point to numerous counterparts of the PLO for acts of terrorism, both near and far. We can also point to endless examples of decent

448

men who were terrorists until they became cured of their frustration and reached positions of responsibility—such as Kenyatta or Mugabe. It will not be helpful to continue seeing all the good in ourselves and all the evil in others.

All those who are not blinded by zealotry are bound to be very unhappy when they realize the terrible acts that have been committed by Israelis—individually and collectively—sometimes in retaliatory raids, sometimes in protective strikes, and sometimes because we have thought it a *mitzvah* to take vengeance on the helpless. Clearly, the PLO has its sadists. And there is indeed the possibility that a PLO state might turn into a Soviet satellite; but who can guarantee that this will not happen to any of our other Arab neighbors? We must avoid pushing the Arabs into a position where they will feel they have suffered so much humiliation that they might as well use all their strength to die with the Palestinians. . . . And yet, we must use our defensive capability to repel all who threaten our existence and seek to destroy us. Ironically, we have worked hard to convince ourselves that there is no possibility of compromise; that the Arabs are implacably resolved to annihilate us, and that we must therefore act accordingly—because we despair of any possibility of peace, or of international guarantees of borders, or of demilitarization arrangements, or of other solutions. I am afraid, Mr. Prime Minister, that this attitude is likely to become a self-fulfilling prophecy.

We should talk with anyone who is prepared to talk with us and, by doing so, is prepared to recognize our existence and our right to be here, and who is willing to declare so on the eve or in the course of the negotiations. I also would not insist on such solemn declarations as a condition for a dialogue. We Jews have learned in the Middle Ages to treat such declarations more like bargaining chips than obligatory expressions of practical intent. In those days, people already distinguished clearly between the sphere of the kingdom of mercy and the eternal sacred values—by which only God, kings, and saints were able to live—and the Vale of Tears where most mortal sinners are bound by laws by which we somehow manage to live. "The Heavens belong to God, and the Earth is mankind's." Let us admit that politics and political arrangements belong to this lower sphere. Let us also admit that it is permissible, and perhaps even desirable, for the sake of aesthetics and conscience, to pay lip service to lofty principles at the beginning of any agreement—so as to alleviate our conscience and to be able to get down to the necessary compromises and pragmatic agreements. Just as humanity cannot survive in laboratory conditions or sustain itself solely on pure substantiality—so we, too, cannot exist in the realm of purism and sheer elevation.

We invite much trouble when we cling to principles as if they were the word of the Living God and, in doing so, we fall in with the fundamentalist zealots. The most famous document in England's diplomatic history was written by Castlereagh, the Conservative counterrevolutionary, and not, as was thought, by the Progressive Canning. It was a response to an invitation to join the Holy Alliance, and it said that England would never undertake any blanket obligations—in this case, to put down rebellions wherever they might occur. England would, instead, deal pragmatically with situations as they came up, and consider each case on its own merits. Some people who once studied law, and who still respect what they then learned, even though they never practiced the legal profession, love to make declarations of rights every other day. This strikes me as political folly. In life, and certainly in political life, we are not interested in narrowly defined rights or principles, but in the conflicts between opposing rights that are in need of compromise, and that require a profound understanding of the prevailing circumstances.

If we accept that the State of Israel and its people now live under a state of siege and are completely isolated; and if we also accept for a moment that Jewry in the Diaspora is eventually bound to disappear; then—given the country's present economic strangulation and its moral and spiritual disintegration—it appears that the Six-Day War was one of Nietzsche's "victories that turn into defeat." The attempt to hold onto the captured territories has turned out to be not the sacred mission that will bring about our redemption and the climax of our history—but a trap, whose burden we cannot withstand without corruption and perhaps even collapse. The world refuses to accept the Revisionist version of Zionism, Mr. Prime Minister, and we do not have the power to force it on them. Nor do we have the strength to establish the "Iron Wall" that Jabotinsky hoped would somehow force the Arabs to accept our existence without losing their self-respect.

Jabotinsky, in contrast to his students, admitted that if "our faith is deep, so is theirs." He refused to believe that they would sell "their country's future" for a mess of pottage; he believed that "any people without exception would fight against the colonization of their country at the hands of people of a different race who come from another country." Balfour was very aware of the contradiction between taking away the right of self-determination from the Arabs of Palestine—and doing so in order to grant the Jewish people a national home. Nonetheless, Balfour was convinced that it was right to ignore the protests of 700,000 Arabs in order to rectify an old historic injustice. At that time, the enlightened world agreed to apply unusual principles to the case of a people that had made a unique contribution to humanity, and had suffered persecution as had no other people in history.

In our situation today, in contrast to what generations have considered our unique gift to humanity—the idea of the rule of the spirit rather than the rule of force—we are using that rule of force. We now are using the rule of force to implement our historic rights; rights that, in their present interpretation, are holy neither to the gentiles nor to most Jews. And so we no longer can expect the world to look upon our rights as so pressing that they ought to cancel out the rights of the Palestinians to self-determination. Without the foundation that is represented by the writings of our prophets, we are nothing but a peculiar band

of tribes that has given nothing to humanity except a lot of trouble, and that is now asking to expand at the expense of another people and to subordinate this other people's freedom to its own security needs, real or imaginary, as well as to its self-interest. . . .

Mr. Prime Minister, the policies of your government are turning the State of Israel into an underground sect; they invite the Jews of the Diaspora to disavow liberal values that have not only made it possible for them to reach positions of unprecedented influence— but values that represent a philosophy to which they are deeply committed. The chauvinist sectarianism that your government is encouraging (and so the version of East European religious orthodoxy to which it has granted special rights while denying such rights to all other forms of Judaism) not only fails to bring our people closer to Judaism; it also harms our people's unity and alienates them from Judaism and from the State of Israel—for the majority of our people will not agree to go back to ghetto life.

The future of Israel and of American Jewry is interconnected. Should, heaven forbid, Judea fall a third time, the Jews of America and of the world will have suffered an overwhelming blow. There would be paralyzing despair, breakdown, and a massive departure from Judaism. Should something fearful happen to American Jewry—despite the calculations of our millenarians who regard anti-Semitism as fuel for Zionism and a supplier of Israel's immigrants—an isolated Israel would not be saved from such a huge conflagration. The future of the entire Jewish people is totally dependent on close cooperations between Israel—as a culture-creating, open, and liberal society—and Diaspora Jewry, particularly American Jewry, some of which today is part of the elite of humanity.

It is not often that a historic problem of a people reaches so dramatic a point that we can characterize it, without exaggeration, with such slogans as that of the French Revolution's "Our country is in danger; help us whoever can!"—or the Russian revolutionaries' call, "Now or never!" You

450

will agree with me, Mr. Prime Minister, that we have reached such a point in our history. Our people now are divided into two camps.

The first camp is convinced there is an international conspiracy to create a PLO state that will be controlled by the Russians and will seek to destroy Israel, and therefore it is imperative to speed up and intensify the settlement process and to pursue an uncompromising policy, inspired by "courageous activism." This camp believes that only thus will catastrophe be averted.

The second camp believes that the moment has come for us to make peace with our neighbors, and that the effort to expand our borders and to force our rule on the population of the territories will dispel all chances for peace, and create dangers for our country from which there can be no salvation.

The adherents of this second camp, Mr. Prime Minister, view your historic achievement of peace negotiations with Egypt as an ambiguous success, while your supporters, the adherents of the first camp, hope that the Camp David agreements, by putting an end to any threat from Egypt, will grant us a free hand to rule over the occupied territories. Your adherents believe that this will lead to the completion of the territorial homeland, that it will grant "personal autonomy" to its Arab residents—confirming Israel's sovereignty and our people's right to settle anywhere within this homeland's borders.

Your opponents, however, are fearful that the other parties to this treaty will continue to view this agreement and the proffered autonomy as nothing but a stage on the way toward guaranteeing a separate Palestinian entity. And your opponents are afraid that the differences of opinion on this issue will intensify the conflict between the Arabs and an Israel that is now weaker as a result of its withdrawal from the Sinai and its oil fields.

I have attempted here, Mr. Prime Minister, to draw your attention to the serious structural changes that have occurred during the decades since the Holocaust in the Jewish population centers that gave birth to Zionism. I have referred to the lack of an effective Zionist response from the Diaspora in the form of mass emigration to Israel. In addition I have tried to outline the recent developments in the larger world, such as decolonization and its ideological and political consequences. I have tried to point also to the rise of civilization and peoples who have no ties to the Bible and feel no obligation toward the Jews. I have also spoken of the important changes that have occurred in the position of the Arab world, thanks to its near-monopoly of the oil resources, which are so vital to our industrial civilization, and of the declining military clout and spiritual strength of the Western nations who are so close to us in tradition and spirit. We must be aware, of course, of the alliance between the Communist ideology (now transformed into the ideology of an imperialist power structure) and the national liberation movements. This alliance has led to the political isolation of the Jewish state and has succeeded in distorting the image of Israel and its historic and moral significance in world public opinion.

Tragically, our victory in the Six-Day War has led our people to a loss of a sense of proportion regarding the strength of the State of Israel, and has shifted too much of our focus upon military matters, away from other significant factors vital to a democratic society. This focus on the military has diverted much of our attention from the nation's economic and social problems—which have to be solved *before* there can be any effective military strength.

So we won on the battlefield but were not strong enough to force our enemy to make peace with us. And the more Israel increased its weaponry, the more dependent it became on American aid and support. Meanwhile, the Palestinians—termed "refugees" in the U.N. Resolution 242—succeeded in obtaining recognition as a people.

Our refusal to treat the Palestinians as a collective entity has diminished Israel's legitimacy in the eyes of the world. And now our people are divided over the meaning and interpretation of the proposed "autonomy." Is it home rule, with selected clerks performing duties that are essentially controlled by the Israeli government? Or is it self-rule, based on partition into two *autonomous* sections, with autonomous authorities in each of them?

Those Israelis who do not believe that the government's autonomy proposals are acceptable to the Arabs of the world are now asking that you preserve the possibility of reaching a real peace settlement. They ask that you preserve the chance for peace by an agreement on territorial autonomy, or even by agreeing to a Palestinian national home in exchange for effective guarantees and a federation with Jordan and a federal tie to Israel. This option seems more promising and less dangerous than the one you have proposed.

The more time passes, the more polarized become both sides, and the Israeli public, too. There is the grave danger of civil war between Jews and Arabs—and Jews and Jews.

Mr. Prime Minister, in the eyes of the majority of the nation, your allegiance to the faith of your youth, and your conviction of having a historic mission to deliver "the home of our fathers" intact to the coming generations appear more and more as an obsession. It seems to be an obsession that has no chance of realization and is a source of errors and disasters that are dividing the nation as well as the Coalition that you lead. Conflicting views, frustrations, and feuds are now paralyzing the operation of that Coalition. They are also destroying the people's respect for its parliamentary institutions, for the democratic process, and for our judicial system and its moral authority. This has led to the creation of extra-parliamentary groups, which now see themselves as agents of the national destiny and the saviors of their people. These groups believe themselves subject only to their own law and rules. . . .

There comes a time in the life of a politician when he must weigh whether, in changing circumstances, he will be an asset or an obstacle in the service of his people. More than one historian has asked in astonishment why, for instance, Lloyd George did not leave political life at the end of his extraordinary historic mission, or why Churchill insisted on remaining on as prime minister for his final term.

What should a leader do who is unable to shake off his youthful faith, even though in their hearts he and others are doubtful that it can be realized? Before him is the example of the Social Democratic leader Philip Scheidemann, the first German chancellor of the Weimar Republic. When the Allies' peace terms of Versailles were announced in 1919, he solemnly swore in an emotional address before the Reichstag: "This hand will not move to sign this disgraceful document!" And Scheidemann resigned. Others were found to sign that document. □

Translated from the Hebrew by Arthur H. Samuelson